2682.4:1

DANIEL WEBSTER

BY

JOHN BACH McMASTER

UNIVERSITY OF PENNSYLVANIA

Illustrated

PUBLIC LIBRARY 41.213

NEW YORK
THE CENTURY CO.
1902

Copyright, 1900, 1901, 1902, by
THE CENTURY CO.

Published October, 1902

THE DE VINNE PRESS.

TO

ROBERT BACH McMASTER

CONTENTS

LIST OF ILLUSTRATIONS

ix

LIST OF ILLUSTRATIONS xi

DANIEL WEBSTER

and-twenty, Ebenezer Webster. He came of a race
of commonwealth-builders who, for a century past,
had lived and fought on the soil of New Hampshire, and was himself a splendid type of sturdy
and vigorous manhood. Born at Kingston, his
youth was passed in the exciting times of King
George's War, when the French and Indians were
harrying the frontier, and when all New England
rang with joy over the capture of the fortress of
Louisburg. He was fifteen when the surrender of
Fort Necessity opened the Seven Years' War in
serious earnest, and before it ended he saw service
that was no child's play in a famous corps known
as Rogers' Rangers.

The war over, Ebenezer Webster came back to
the settlements, selected Stevenstown as his future
home, took up land, and built a log cabin, to which,
a year later, he brought a wife. The town was
then on the very edge of the frontier, and as his
cabin was farther north than any other, not a habitation save those of the red man lay between him
and Canada. In this wilderness home five children
were born before the mother died, after ten years
of wedded life, and the father brought to it as his
second wife Abigail Eastman.

Wringing a livelihood from such a soil in such
a climate was hard enough at any time, but the task
was now made more difficult still by the opening
of the long struggle between the colonies and the
mother-country, and the constant demand on his

DANIEL WEBST

CHAPTER I

SCHOOL DAYS

ONE hundred and fifty years ago, when Ne,
Hampshire was a royal province, when the
frontier of civilization had not been pushed farther
up the Merrimac than Concord, when the French
still held the Mississippi valley, the Great Lakes,
and the river St. Lawrence, and were about to
build their forts at the headwaters of the Alleghany, when events were hurrying on the seven
years' struggle that was to settle once and for all
who should rule America, a band of hardy pio-
neers took up land under patent, and, in the heart
of the forest, some eighteen miles north of Concord, laid the foundation of Major Stevens' town.

The venture was scarcely started when the storm
of war burst upon the country, and not until the
victory on the Plains of Abraham gave peace and
quiet to the frontier did Stevenstown, soon re-
named Salisbury, begin to thrive. Another band
of backwoodsmen then made it their home, and
among these was a young Indian-fighter of four-

"WEBSTER'S HOUSE," DARTMOUTH COLLEGE, WHERE DANIEL
WEBSTER ROOMED WHEN A STUDENT.

time for services, both civil and military. Now we see him, after the fights at Concord and Lexington, hurrying at the head of his company to join the forces around Boston; now home again to serve as delegate to the convention which framed the first constitution of New Hampshire. Now we see him, a true minuteman, resigning his captaincy and hastening to serve under Washington, in an hour of dire need at White Plains; then home again to become a member of a committee to prevent forestalling and to regulate the prices of commodities. Now we behold him at the head of seventy men pushing through the wilderness for the relief of Ticonderoga; now returning when he hears of the evacuation of the fort, and reaching home just in time to lead back another band that fought gallantly at Bennington. Once again at home we find him at the head of more committees to regulate prices, to enlist the town's quota for the Continental army, and finally in command of four companies raised to aid in the defense of West Point. Public services of such various sorts bespeak a man with a will not easily bent, with a capacity to do equal to any emergency, with a patriotism rising above all considerations of self; a man courageous, resourceful, self-reliant, and commanding the entire confidence and respect of his fellows.

By the time Cornwallis surrendered and the fighting ended, three more children had been added to the little flock. The log cabin had now become too small, and a farm-house was built near by. It was the typical New England farm-house of the day—one story high, clapboarded, with the chimney in the center, the door in the middle of the south side, four rooms on the ground floor, and a lean-to in the rear for a kitchen; and in this house, on January 18, 1782, another son was born, and named Daniel.

When the child was a year and more old the parents moved to the banks of the Merrimac, to Elms Farm, a place of some local interest, for on it, within a cabin whose site was plainly visible in Webster's day, had been perpetrated one of the many Indian massacres that make up so much of frontier history, and near this had stood one of the last of the forts built to protect the inhabitants of Salisbury and the neighboring towns against the savages.

As the boy grew in years and stature his life was powerfully affected by the facts that he was the youngest son and ninth child in a family of ten; that his health was far from good; that he showed tastes and mental traits that stood out in marked contrast with those of his brothers and sisters; and that he was, from infancy, the pet of the family. Such daily work as a farmer's lad was then made to do was not for him. Yet he was expected to do something, and might have been seen barefooted, in frock and trousers, astride of the horse that dragged the plow between the rows of corn, or raking hay, or binding the wheat the reapers cut, or following the cows to pasture in the morning and home again at night, or tending logs in his father's sawmill. When such work was to be done it was his custom to take a book along, set the log, hoist the gates, and while the saw passed slowly through the tree-trunk, an operation which, in those days, consumed some twenty minutes, he would settle himself comfortably and read.

He was taught to read, he tells us, by his mother and sister at so early an age that he never knew the time when he could not peruse the Bible with ease. With this humble beginning, his further education was intrusted to the village schoolmaster. The town of Salisbury was then so divided for school purposes that the district in which Webster lived stretched away from the Merrimac River to the hills several miles off, and had within it three rude log school-houses. One stood near the river-bank, another was on the old North Road, and the third in the west end of the township. So little was there attractive in this backwoods community that the wandering schoolmaster seems never to have visited it, and his place was filled by some humble resident who added to the profits of his farm or his store by keeping the district schools, teaching spelling, reading, writing, and arithmetic for a few weeks each year, and receiving in return the pittance of a few dollars. It was in the shop kept by one of these teachers that Dan-

iel, while still a mere child, first beheld a copy of
the Federal Constitution, printed with gorgeous
adornment on a cotton pocket-handkerchief. Attracted probably by the eagle, the flags, and the
brilliant coloring, he bought the handkerchief, read
the text, and "from this," says he, "I learned
either that there was a constitution or that there
were thirteen States."

Most parents were then content to send their
boys and girls to school when it was kept in the
house nearest their homes. But the father of Daniel was determined to give his son the best education the land afforded, so he was made to follow
the master from place to place. When school was
held in the middle house, but a few miles off, he
walked to and fro each day; when at the western
end of the district, Daniel was boarded out in
some family near by. When no schooling was to
be had the boy roamed the woods and fields with
a rough old British sailor who taught him to row
and to fish, and filled his head with stories of
bloody fights and strange adventures on land and
sea. For Jack had served under Admiral Byng
in the Mediterranean; had deserted from the garrison at Gibraltar; had wandered through Spain,
France, and Holland; had been arrested and sent
back to the army; had fought at Meriden; had
come over to Boston with Gage; had thrice
marched up Bunker Hill on the ever-memorable
day in June; had deserted to the Continentals; had

enlisted in a New Hampshire regiment, and, the war over, had built a little cabin on one corner of the Elms Farm.

In 1791, when Daniel had just turned nine, a new honor which deeply affected his later career came to his father. The many evidences of confidence and esteem a grateful community had bestowed on Ebenezer Webster in the dark days of the Revolution did not cease with the war. The leader in strife remained a leader in peace, was sent year after year first to one and then to the other branch of the Assembly, was a delegate to the convention which ratified the Federal Constitution, and finally, in 1791, was placed on the bench of the Court of Common Pleas for the county in which he resided. These courts were composed of a presiding judge, always an able lawyer, and two side justices, usually laymen of hard common sense and sterling integrity; and it was to one of these side justiceships that Ebenezer Webster was appointed. The office was one of honor and dignity, and carried with it an annual salary of several hundred dollars, just enough to enable the father to go on with his long-meditated plan for the education of Daniel.

- Of his five sons, Ebenezer, David, and Joseph had grown to manhood, were settled in life, and long past the school age. To educate the two remaining, Ezekiel and Daniel, was beyond his means. But if his longing to see at least one son rise above the humble calling of a farmer was to be gratified, it must be one of these, and to choose which cost the father a bitter struggle. He met it with the unfaltering courage which marked the man, made his decision, and one day in 1795 announced his determination. "On a hot day in July," said Webster, describing the scene many years later, "it must have been in one of the last years of Washington's administration, I was making hay with my father, just where I now see a remaining elm-tree. About the middle of the forenoon the Hon. Abiel Foster, M.C., who lived in Canterbury, six miles off, called at the house and came into the field to see my father. When he was gone my father called me to him, and we sat down beneath the elm on a haycock. He said: 'My son, that is a worthy man; he is a member of Congress; he goes to Philadelphia and gets six dollars a day, while I toil here. It is because he had an education which I never had. If I had had his education I should have been in Philadelphia in his place. I came near it as it was. But I missed it, and now I must work here.' 'My dear father,' said I, 'you shall not work; brother and I will work for you, and we will wear our hands out, and you shall rest.' And I remember to have cried, and I cry now at the recollection. 'My child,' said he, 'it is of no importance to me. I now live but for my children. I could not give your elder brothers the advantages of knowledge, but I can do something for you. Exert yourself, improve your oppor-

REV. JOSEPH STEVENS BUCKMINSTER.

tunities, learn, learn, and when I am gone you will
not need to go through the hardships which I have
undergone, and which have made me an old man
before my time.' "

Almost a year passed, however, before the plan
so long cherished was fairly started, and Daniel,
dressed in a brand-new home-made suit and astride
a side-saddle, rode with his father to Exeter to
be entered at the famous academy founded by
John Phillips. The principal then and forty years
thereafter was Dr. Benjamin Abbot, one of the
greatest teachers our country has yet produced.
As the doctor was ill, the duty of examining the
new pupil fell to Joseph S. Buckminster, then an
usher at the academy, but destined to influence
strongly the religious life of New England. It was
the custom of the doctor, we are told, to conduct
the examination of applicants with pompous cere-
mony, and that, imitating him, young Buckminster
summoned Webster to his presence, put on his hat,
and said, "Well, sir, what is your age?" "Fourteen," was the reply. "Take this Bible, my lad,
and read that chapter." The passage given him
was St. Luke's dramatic description of the conspir-
ing of Judas with the chief priests and scribes, of
the Last Supper, of the betrayal by Judas, of the
three denials of Peter, and of the scene in the house
of the high priest. But young Webster was equal
to the test, and read the whole passage to the end
in a voice and with a fervor such as Master Buck-

minster had never listened to before. "Young man," said he, "you are qualified to enter this institution," and no more questions were put by him. The voice and manner so famous in later life were even then strikingly manifest. But one other gift of nature still lay dormant—he could not declaim. Long after he had become the greatest orator of the day he said to a friend: "I could not speak before the school. Many a piece did I commit to memory and rehearse in my room over and over again, but when the day came, and the schoolmaster called my name, and I saw all eyes turned upon my seat, I could not raise myself from it. When the occasion was over I went home and wept bitter tears of mortification."

His stay at the academy was short. At the close of the year he was home again, teaching a small class of boys and girls at his uncle's house on the North Road, and while so engaged he made the acquaintance of the Rev. Samuel Wood, minister at Boscawen, some six miles from Salisbury. But Dr. Wood was more than a minister: he was an educator, and in the course of a pastorate covering nearly half a century taught in his own house, often without remuneration and sometimes at the cost of board and lodgings, one hundred and fifty-five young men. That so promising a lad as Webster should be cut short in his school career seemed a pity, and arming himself with the testimony of Dr. Abbot, he went to Colonel Webster, said what he thought, urged that the boy be sent to college, and offered to fit him. Nothing was closer to the father's heart, and the next few months were spent in the house of Dr. Wood.

The doctor took charge of his Latin; a young senior from Dartmouth taught him some Greek; and in August, 1797, Webster became a freshman in Dartmouth College, more through the influence of Trustee Wood than by merit. He had now reached a turning-point in his career. Save during the nine months spent at Phillips Exeter, he had never been so far from home, had never been so completely thrown on his own resources, nor brought in close contact with so many young men of his own age and generation. He was free to make of himself what he pleased, and acted accordingly, following the path of least resistance. Greek and mathematics he disliked and shunned; but he read widely in English literature and in history, acquired a familiarity with Latin and with Latin authors, never forgot anything once acquired, was always able to display his knowledge to the best advantage, was in no sense a student or a scholar, but became the best-informed man in college, and impressed all who met him as a youth of uncommon parts, with promise of being a great man. "So much as I read," says he, "I made my own. When a half-hour, or an hour at most, had elapsed, I closed my book, and thought over what I had read. If there was anything peculiarly interesting or striking in the passage, I endeavored to recall it and lay it up in my memory, and commonly could effect my object. Then if, in debate or conversation afterward, any subject came up on which I had read something, I could talk very easily so far as I had read, and there I was very careful to stop."

As time passed, this wide reading stood him in good stead, and for a year he paid his board by aiding in editing a weekly newspaper for which he made selections from books and contemporary publications, now and then writing a few paragraphs himself. Nor were his physical characteristics less striking. College mates never forgot his deep-set eyes, the solemn tones of his voice, the dignity of his carriage, and, above all, his eloquence. The old shyness that tormented him so at the academy was gone. At last the greatest of his natural gifts was developing rapidly and was used freely. At first his audience was the Society of the United Fraternity; but his fame spread, and when the people of Hanover were casting about for an orator to speak to them on the Fourth of July, 1800, they turned with one accord to young Webster.

Judged by the side of his later efforts, the oration delivered on that day was indeed a weak and school-boy production. Yet it is not beneath the vast mass of patriotic speeches to which our forefathers gladly listened, on fast-days and Thanks-

THE SECOND ACADEMY BUILDING (PHILLIPS EXETER ACADEMY), AS IT
STOOD WHEN ATTENDED BY DANIEL WEBSTER IN 1796.
DANIEL WEBSTER'S HOUSE IN PORTSMOUTH, NEW HAMPSHIRE.

giving days, on the 22d of every February and the 4th of every July, and it richly deserved the honor of publication.

There is plenty of that sort of rhetoric which was the fashion of the day, and without which any speech, in the opinion of the crowd, would have been but a poor affair. Washington was the man who "never felt a wound but when it pierced his country, who never groaned but when fair freedom bled." Napoleon is "the gasconading pilgrim of Egypt, who will never dictate terms to sovereign America." Great Britain is "haughty Albion." Columbia is now seated "in the forum of the nations, and the empires of the world are amazed at the bright effulgence of her glory." The cannon of our navy is to "fulminate destruction on Frenchmen till the ocean is crimsoned with blood and gorged with pirates." But the bombast detracts in no wise from our interest in the speech. On that day, for the first time in his life, Webster spoke to a popular audience, and to the political doctrine then announced he ever remained faithful. Love of country, devotion to the Union, the grandeur of the Constitution, and the blessings of a free government administered by the people, made his theme. No question of State rights troubled him. "In the adoption of our present systems of jurisprudence," said he, "we see the powers necessary for government voluntarily flowing from the people, their only origin, and directed to the public good, their only proper object." It was the people of these States "who engaged in the transaction which is undoubtedly the greatest approach toward human perfection the political world ever yet witnessed, and which, perhaps, will forever stand in the history of mankind without a parallel."

This was rank Federalism; but that the lad should be a Federalist was inevitable. He had been reared at the knee of a man who had fought and toiled and spent his substance in the strugg. for independence, who had followed the leadership of Washington in peace with the same unfaltering loyalty that he had followed it in war, and had received from his father a political creed of no uncertain kind. Since coming to years of discretion nothing had occurred to weaken, but much to strengthen, the belief so inherited. He had seen a foreign power meddling in our domestic affairs, had read the letter in which Adet threatened the vengeance of France if Mr. Jefferson were not elected, and had since beheld that insolent threat made good. He had seen our minister to the French republic rejected, the X. Y. Z. commissioners insulted, and the whole country roused to indignation and ringing with the cry: "Millions for defense, but not a cent for tribute." He had seen a provisional army raised and Washington put in command; he had seen the young men associate for defense, and the old men once again mount the black cockade of the Revolution, as an open defiance to those who, to their shame, wore the tricolor of France; he had seen seaport after seaport arm and equip a vessel of war, and had beheld the little navy so created triumph over every foe and bring France at last to reason.

All these things, in his opinion, took place because a large part of his countrymen had been deaf to the advice of Washington, had quit their own to stand on foreign ground, and had formed in America a party warmly devoted to France. "But why," he asked, "shall every quarrel on the other side of the Atlantic interest us in its issue? Why shall the rise or depression of every party there produce here a corresponding vibration? Was this continent designed as a mere satellite to the other? Has not nature here wrought all operations on her broadest scale? The natural superiority of America clearly indicates that it was designed to be inhabited by a nobler race of men, possessing a superior form of government, superior patriotism, superior talents, and superior virtues. Let, then, the nations of the East muster their strength in destroying each other. Let them aspire to conquest and contend for dominion till their continent is deluged in blood. But let none, however elated by victory, however proud of triumph, ever presume to intrude on the neutral position assumed by our country." A little later these ideas found expression in the Monroe Doctrine.

2

CHAPTER II

STRUGGLING WITH POVERTY AND LAW

THE year after the Hanover speech Webster was graduated from Dartmouth, and went back to his father's farm, there to decide the hardest question he had yet encountered; for he was to make up his mind what he would do for a living, and how he must set about the doing of it. No strong taste, no feeling of special fitness for anything, guided him in his choice, and with much reluctance and great indifference he finally entered the office of Thomas W. Thompson and began the study of law, where, six years before, as a barefoot urchin of thirteen, he had served as office-boy and told the clients when they called where Mr. Thompson was to be found.

"I have precipitated myself in an office," he wrote to his friend Bingham, "with how much prudence I do not allow myself to think. I am not, like you, harassed with dreams, nor troubled with any waverings of inclination; but am rather sunken in indifference and apathy." To another friend he wrote: "I fell into a law office, pretty much by casualty, after commencement, where I am at pres-

24

ent. Considering how long I must read, prospects are not very flattering, but perhaps I may find room hereafter, in some wilderness where the violet has not resigned her tenement, to make writs without disturbance of rivals if there should be nobody to purchase.''

In Mr. Thompson's office Webster thus fairly started on his career, read Vattel, Montesquieu, and Blackstone, the histories of Robertson and Hume, and was deep in the plays of Shakspere and the poetry of Milton, Cowper, and Pope, when his studies were suddenly cut short by the dire need of money. Yielding to his earnest pleadings, his father, who indeed ''lived but for his children,'' had consented that Ezekiel should have the same chance in the world that had been given to him, and the lad had entered Dartmouth College. But the family treasury was empty. Money must be had, and to get it Daniel once more became a teacher, accepted the charge of an academy, and having purchased a horse and stuffed his saddle-bags with clothes and books, rode across country to the little town of Fryeburg, Maine. His salary was to be three hundred and fifty dollars a year; but the county register, with whom he boarded, gave him the work of copying deeds sent to be recorded, and so enabled him to earn a trifle more. Of a long winter's evening he could copy two deeds, for which he was paid fifty cents. ''Four evenings in a week,'' says he, ''I earned two dollars,'' and one dollar and three quarters ''a week paid my board.'' But it did more: it enabled him to save every cent of salary, and at the end of the first quarter he rode across the hills to Hanover and put all of it into the hands of his brother for college expenses.

After teaching for nine months at Fryeburg, Webster went back to the study of law at Salisbury. The academy trustees would gladly have retained him, and offered nearly twice the old salary, a house, and a plot of ground; and, what was quite as alluring, a clerkship in the Court of Common Pleas seemed quite within reach. For a time he was sorely tempted.

''What shall I do?'' he wrote. ''Shall I say, 'Yes, gentlemen,' and sit down here to spend my days in a kind of comfortable privacy, or shall I relinquish these prospects and enter into a profession where my feelings will be constantly harrowed by objects either of dishonesty or misfortune; where my living must be squeezed from penury (for rich folks seldom go to law), and my moral principle continually be at hazard? I agree with you that the law is well calculated to draw forth the powers of the mind, but what are its effects on the heart; are they equally propitious? Does it inspire benevolence and awake tenderness; or does it, by a frequent repetition of wretched objects, blunt sensibility and stifle the still, small voice of mercy?

"The talent with which heaven has intrusted me is small, very small, yet I feel responsible for the use of it, and am not willing to pervert it to purposes reproachful or unjust, nor to hide it, like the slothful servant, in a napkin.

"Now I will enumerate the inducements that draw me toward the law. First, and principally, it is my father's wish. He does not dictate, it is true, but how much short of dictation is the mere wish of a parent whose labors of life are wasted on favors to his children? Even the delicacy with which this wish is expressed gives it more effect than it would have in the form of a command. Secondly, my friends generally wish it. They are urgent and pressing. My father even offers me— I will sometime tell you what—and Mr. Thompson offers my tuition gratis, and to relinquish his stand to me.

"On the whole, I imagine I shall make one more trial in the ensuing autumn." In the end the father's wish prevailed, and he was soon back again in the office of Mr. Thompson, struggling with poverty, eager for a wider field of action, and longing for the day to come when some "miracle," as he said, would enable him to finish his studies in Boston.

His poverty at this time was dire. At the close of his service in the Fryeburg Academy, when all his savings had gone to aid Ezekiel, he writes to a friend: "You will naturally inquire how I prosper

in the articles of cash. Finely! finely! I came here
in January with a horse and watch, etc., and a
few 'rascally counters' in my pocket. Was soon
obliged to sell my horse and live on the proceeds.
Still straitened for cash, I sold my watch, and
made a shift to get home, where my friends supplied me with another horse and another watch.
My horse is sold again, and my watch goes, I expect, this week; thus you see how I lay up cash.''

After his return to Salisbury he writes to his
brother: ''Now, Zeke, you will not read half a sentence, no, not one syllable, before you have thoroughly searched this sheet for scrip; but, my word
for it, you will find no scrip here. We held a san-
hedrim this morning on the subject of cash; could
not hit upon any way to get you any; just before
we went away to hang ourselves through disappointment, it came into our heads that next week
might do. . . .

''I have now by me two cents in lawful Federal
currency; next week I will send them, if they be
all; they will buy a pipe; with a pipe you can
smoke; smoking inspires wisdom; wisdom is allied
to fortitude; from fortitude it is but one step to
stoicism, and stoicism never pants for this world's
goods; so perhaps my two cents, by this process,
may put you quite at ease about cash.'' While
this letter was on its way to Hanover, Ezekiel, who
was much in need of a ''warm greatcoat,'' of any
kind or color of cloth, provided it would ''keep

the frost out," wrote: "Money, Daniel, money. As I was walking down to the office after a letter, I happened to find one cent, which is the only money I have had since the second day after I came on. It is a fact, Dan, that I was called on for a dollar where I owed it, and borrowed it, and have borrowed it four times since to pay those I borrowed of."

What should be Webster's life work was now settled; but he had still to decide where he could perform it, and a long list of places was passed in review. To his friend James Bingham, who wrote to ask if it were true that he was to settle in Vermont, he replied: "My father has an important suit at law pending before the Supreme Court of Vermont. This has frequently called me into that realm in the course of the past summer. Mr. Marsh of Woodstock is of counsel to us, wherefore I have made him several visits in arranging the necessary preliminaries to trial. This circumstance, I fancy, originated the suggestion that I contemplated reading in his office. In reality, I have no such idea in my head at present. Heretofore I have been inclined to think of Vermont as a place of practice, and as preparatory therefor have thought it possible that I might read a year in that State; but I never carried my views so far as to fix on an office, and at this time have no views at all of that kind.

"Secondly. You have heard that I contemplated finishing my studies in Massachusetts.

There is more foundation for this than the other. It is true I have laid many plans to enable myself to be some time in Boston before I go into practice, but I did not know that I had mentioned the circumstance abroad, because it is all uncertain. I believe that some acquaintance in the capital of New England would be very useful to us who expect to plant ourselves down as country lawyers. But I cannot control my fortune; I must follow wherever circumstances lead. My going to Boston is therefore much more a matter of hope than of probability; unless something like a miracle puts the means in my hands, I shall not budge from here very soon. Depend on it, however, James, that I shall sometime avail myself of more advantages than this smoky village affords. But when and where you and I know equally well. If my circumstances were like yours, I would by all means pass a six months in Boston. The acquaintances you would be like to form there might help you to much business in the course of life. You can pass that time there just as well as not, and I therefore advise to it, as far as I ought to advise to anything. But 'some men are born with a silver spoon in their mouths, and others with a wooden ladle.' "

A little later, in March of 1804, he confides to the same friend the fact that "several gentlemen of the profession have mentioned to me two or three towns, in Cheshire County, where an industrious young man might probably make a moderate living. Washington, Westmoreland, and Chesterfield have been named. As to the first, if you settle at Lempster, as I suppose you will, it will be too near to you; so let that go. The other two I wish you to write to me about as particularly as you can. I know I am in great season, as I have a year longer to read, but there are some other reasons which induce me to wish to know generally what part of the country I shall inhabit. It is more than probable that I shall be leaving this place in April or May. If I could think it likely that I should hereafter find a resting-place at some town in Cheshire, I should be fond of reading in that quarter awhile. Now you know, if I could have my wish, I should be as fond of being in Mr. West's office as anywhere. Silence! Don't whisper a word; don't ever think aloud, but ponder these matters a little at the bottom of your heart and write me. Inquire if any charitable, clever fellow at Charlestown would keep me and get his pay when he could. Utter not a word for the soul of you, but let me hear from you forthwith."

His friend having made the inquiry, and having answered that "Mr. West leaves the matter with me," Webster replied:

"I am now going, James, to give you a full survey of the 'whole ground' as it respects my prospects, hopes, and wishes. The great object of a lawyer is business; but this is not, or ought not to be, his sole object. Pleasant society, an agreeable acquaintance, and a degree of respectability not merely as a lawyer, but as a man, are other objects of importance. You and I commenced the study, you know, with a resolution, which we did not say much about, of being honest and conscientious practitioners. Some part of this resolution is, I hope, still hanging about me, and for this reason I choose to settle in a place where the practice of the bar is fair and honorable. The Cheshire bar, as far as I have learned, is entitled to a preference in these respects over that of any county in the State. You know my partiality for Connecticut River folks generally. Their information and habits are far better, in my opinion, than those of the people in the eastern part of the State. These reasons compel me to say with you, 'it is a goodly land,' and to make it my wish to settle therein.

"*E contra.* Many of my friends are desirous that I should make an attempt to live in Portsmouth. Mr. Thompson, my good master, knows everything about the comparative advantages of different places everywhere in New Hampshire, except Cheshire County. He has frequently suggested to me that Portsmouth would be a good place for a young man; and the other evening, when I hinted my inclination for Cheshire, he said he had a high esteem for the people that way, but added that he still wished me to consider Portsmouth. He says there are many gentlemen of char-

acter there who would patronize a young lawyer,
and thinks that even Mr. Attorney-General would
be fond of the thing.

"Mr. T. will have business on which I shall be at
Portsmouth as soon as the roads are passable, and,
out of respect to his opinion, I shall make no certain arrangements for my future reading till that
time. At present I do not feel that Portsmouth is
the place for me."

In this state of uncertainty Daniel turned next
to his brother, then teaching school in Boston.
"Agreeably to your injunction," said Ezekiel, "I
have thought and meditated upon your letter for
three days and for no inconsiderable portion of
three nights, and I now give you the results as
freely as I earnestly wish your welfare. I am directly opposed to your going to New York, and for
several reasons. First, the expensiveness of a journey to that city and of a residence in it is, with me,
a material objection. Secondly, the embarrassments to which you will be liable without friends
to assist or patronage to support you. Thirdly, I
fear the climate would be injurious to your constitution. I have now told you what I would not
have you do, and I also tell you what I wish you
to do. I would have you decamp immediately,
with all your baggage, from Salisbury, and march
directly to this place. This is the opinion I have
maturely formed, for which a thousand reasons
might be urged. They are too numerous to be

mentioned, nor is it perhaps necessary, for I say to you imperatively, 'Come.' It is the easiest thing in the world for a fellow of any enterprise or ability to support himself here, very handsomely, without descending to any business incompatible with the situation of a gentleman. Here, too, is the focus of information. Any person, however stupid and inefficient, cannot but learn something. With a head ever so impenetrable, some ideas will penetrate it. I will state to you a single circumstance which, I think, will remove all doubt about paying your way. I have now eight scholars in Latin and Greek whom I shall be obliged to dismiss if I cannot have an assistant, and I dare not at present hire one. The tuition of these eight scholars will pay for your board. They recite twice in a day, and it will take you about three fourths of an hour to hear them each time. Here, then, you can support yourself by the labor of one hour and a half each day. If you will spend that time in my school daily, I will board you at as genteel a boarding-house as you can wish or the place affords. Consult father, the family, and your friends, and start for Boston the next day after the receipt of this letter. Another such an opportunity may never occur. Come, and if you don't find everything to your liking, I will carry you back to Salisbury with a chaise and six, and pay you for your time. I must say again, consult father; if he approves, take the patriarchal blessing and come.''

This advice Daniel decided to take, and promptly replied: "Salisbury, you perceive, as yet heads my letters, and how much longer it may I can hardly tell. I know it is much better for me to be absent, and I am zealously laboring to put myself into a new situation. If I recollect, I informed you my intention was to depart as soon as it is possible for me to get a little cash to enable me to rig out; for when I leave this vale, emphatically a 'vale of tears,' I am determined to be under no obligations to anybody in the neighborhood except those of gratitude and friendship. I never heard what particular substance Archimedes wished his desired fulcrum to be, resting on which he was going to move the world; but if his design had been to move everything in it, he would have wished it cash; of all things of a perishable nature, it is worth the most. It ever did, does now, and ever will constitute the real, unavoidable aristocracy that exists and must exist in society. I had an expectation of putting into execution a plan that would have made me able to see you immediately. It was well laid, and I begged of father to attend to it last week at court, but he forgot it."

The plan was, of course, to borrow money, and, having failed, a month and more sped by before he was able to write:

"Day after to-morrow, if the wind blows from the right point, I start for East Andover; on this tour I expect to be absent about twelve days, and soon after my return here I expect to be in Bos-

ton. The season is now so far advanced, I intend
to make my calculation so as to be merely season-
able in town, to learn the arrangements of your
school and be able to manage it till you go after
your degree. Now, I want you to be particular.
Some time ago you mentioned to me a few Latin
and Greek scholars; since then you keep glued lips
on the subject of your school. I desire to know
whether you can employ me, how many hours per
day, in what doing, and for what reward? All
these questions you must certainly answer, and
have your answers here by the time I return. Tell
me into whose office I had better go; whether letters of introduction, and from whom, would be useful; in short, tell me everything.''

The plan thus formed was firmly held to, and
one day in July, 1804, Webster entered Boston,
and set off, without friends or even letters of introduction, to find an office in which to study. The
youth who had given his school to Ezekiel went
along, and in the course of their search they presented themselves one day to Mr. Christopher
Gore, told him that Webster was from the country,
had studied law, had come to Boston to work, not
to play, was most desirous to be his pupil, and
asked that a place be kept for him till letters could
be had from New Hampshire. Impressed by the
presence and seriousness of the unknown youth,
Mr. Gore talked with Webster awhile, and when
he was about to go said: ''You look as though

CHRISTOPHER GORE.

you might be trusted. You say you come to study, not to waste time. I will take you at your word. You may hang up your hat at once and write at your convenience to New Hampshire for your letters.'' Describing the scene in a letter, Webster declares that when he was introduced by his friend, who was as much a stranger as he to Mr. Gore, his name was pronounced indistinctly, and that he was a week in the office before Mr. Gore knew what to call him. ''This,'' he said, ''I call setting out in the world. But I most devoutly hope that I shall never have to set out again.''

The acquaintance thus begun fast ripened into a friendship, of which Mr. Gore soon gave a signal proof. The clerk of the Court of Common Pleas, of which Ebenezer Webster was a side justice, having died, the chief justice promptly tendered the office to Daniel. The place yielded, in fees, some fifteen hundred dollars a year, a sum sufficient to enable him to raise the load of family debt, make his father's last days comfortable, be independent, help Ezekiel, and in time lift the mortgage on the farm. Overjoyed at such good fortune, he hurried with the news to Mr. Gore, who astonished him with the remark, ''You don't mean to accept it, surely.'' ''I told him,'' says Webster, ''as soon as I could speak, that I had no thought of anything else. 'Well,' said he, 'you must decide for yourself; but come, sit down, and let us talk it over. The office is worth fifteen hundred dollars a year, you say.

Well, it will never be worth any more. Ten to one, if they find out it is so much, the fees will be reduced. You are appointed now by friends; others may fill their places who are of different opinions, and who have friends of their own to provide for. You will lose your place; or, supposing you do retain it, what are you but a clerk for life? Go on, and finish your studies; you are poor enough, but there are greater evils than poverty. Live on no man's favor. What bread you eat, let it be the bread of independence.' "

Webster had now reached another turning-point in his career. The temptation to accept the clerkship was great. "Here," said he, "was present comfort, competency, and, I may even say, riches, as I then viewed things, all ready to be enjoyed, and I was called upon to reject them for the uncertain and distant prospect of professional success." But the advice of Mr. Gore was sound, and was taken, to the bitter regret of the father, whose heart was set on seeing his son clerk of the court. He had long had the office in view for Daniel; to disappoint him was hard, but it had to be done, and Webster with a heavy heart went home to do it. "I got home," he said, when describing the scene in after years, "one afternoon, just after sunset, and saw my father in his little room, sitting in his arm-chair. He was pretty old then. His face was pale and his cheeks sunken, and his eyes, which were always very large and black, seemed

larger and blacker than I ever saw them. He
seemed glad to see me, and almost as soon as I sat
down he said: 'Well, Daniel, we have got that office
for you.' 'Yes, father,' said I. 'The gentlemen
were very kind. I must go and thank them.'
'They gave it to you without my saying a word
about it.' 'I must go and see Judge Farrar, and
tell him I am much obliged to him.' And so I
talked about it very carelessly, and tried to make
my father understand me. At last he began to
have some suspicion of what I meant, and he
straightened himself up in his chair, and looked
at me as though he would look me through. 'Daniel, Daniel,' said he, 'don't you mean to take that
office?' 'No, indeed, father,' said I; 'I hope I can
do better than that. I mean to use my tongue in
the courts, not my pen; to be an orator, not a register of other men's acts.' For a moment I thought
he was angry. He looked at me for as much as
a minute, and then said very slowly: 'Well, my
son, your mother has always said you would come
to something or nothing, she was not sure which.
I think you are now about settling that doubt for
her.' "

Having thus announced his purpose to be a
lawyer, not a clerk, Webster went back to the office
of Mr. Gore, was admitted to practice in the Court
of Common Pleas in Boston in March, 1805, and
opened an office in the little town of Boscawen, hard
by Elms Farm, that he might be near his father.

3

"You must know," he wrote to his friend Bingham, "that I have opened a shop in this village for the manufacture of justice writs. Other mechanics do pretty well here, and I am determined to try my luck among others. March 25 I left Boston, with a good deal of regret, I assure you. I was then bound for Portsmouth; but I found my father extremely ill and little fit to be left by all his sons, and therefore, partly through duty, partly through necessity, and partly through choice, I concluded to make my stand here."

Another letter tells of his success. "It is now eight months since I opened an office in this town, during which time I have led a life which I know not how to describe better than by calling it a life of writs and summonses. Not that I have dealt greatly in those articles, but that I have done little else. My business has been just about so so; its quantity less objectionable than its quality. I shall be able at the end of the year to pay my bills and pay perhaps sixty pounds for my books. I practise in Hillsborough, Rockingham, and Grafton. . . . Last year I wrote a pamphlet in two days, which I have the pleasure of seeing kicked about under many tables. But you are one of the very few who know the author of the 'Appeal to the Old Whigs.' "

At Boscawen Webster lived for two years and more, found plenty of time to read and study, added still more to his reputation as a public

WEBSTER'S MOTHER.

PUBLIC LIBRARY
Portland, Me.
41.2 13

speaker, and wrote a couple of essays for the "Monthly Anthology," a Boston magazine from which the present "North American Review" is descended.

Concerning his work as a lawyer, innumerable traditions have come down to us. One presents him as arguing his first case before the court of which his father was a judge. Another pictures him as pleading a cause so ably before the chief justice that his Honor remarked, on leaving the court-house, that he had "never before met such a young man as that." A third recalls a famous murder trial in the course of which Webster astonished all present by his deep insight into the workings of the human mind, and depicted the infirmities of human nature with such eloquence that the jury and the bystanders were moved to tears. These tales were told long after Mr. Webster had become famous, and are to be treated accordingly. That he was a good lawyer with a steadily growing practice, was an effective public speaker, and had won no little local fame before removing to Portsmouth, is all that is certain.

This removal took place in 1807. His father was then dead, and feeling no longer bound to waste his energies on the petty business of a country attorney, Daniel made over his office to Ezekiel, and during nine years was a citizen in the great seaport and chief town of New Hampshire. While living in Portsmouth he married Miss Grace

Fletcher, who became the mother of his five children: a daughter, Grace, who died while a girl; a son, Daniel Fletcher; a daughter, Julia; a son, Edward, who died of disease in the Mexican War; and a son, Charles, who died while an infant.

From a business standpoint the change was most fortunate. The cases that came to him were far more important than any in Boscawen. They brought him in contact with the great lawyers of the State, called forth his best efforts, and made him more widely known. At Boscawen and Salisbury he was by far the most eloquent speaker, the ablest lawyer, the brightest young man in the community, and had very naturally formed an estimate of himself which neither his years nor his experience justified. But at Portsmouth he soon found himself contending with lawyers who could and did teach him much that he had the good sense to learn.

A story is told of an early encounter with William Plumer, then a senator from New Hampshire, and one of the best lawyers in the State, which well illustrates Webster's youthful manner. In the course of an argument, Mr. Plumer cited a few lines from a book called "Peake's Law of Evidence," whereupon Webster scoffed at the passage as bad law, ridiculed the book as a wretched compilation, and, throwing it down upon the table, exclaimed: "So much for Mr. Thomas Peake's compendium of the Law of Evidence." But Mr.

GRACE FLETCHER (MRS. DANIEL WEBSTER).

Plumer, not at all abashed, quietly produced a volume of reports, read from it the despised passage, and informed the court that it was taken word for word from one of Lord Mansfield's decisions.

The man who at this time influenced Webster most powerfully was Jeremiah Mason, one of the greatest masters of common law our country has produced. "If anybody," said he, "should think I was somewhat familiar with the law on some points, and should be curious enough to desire to know how it happened, tell him that Jeremiah Mason compelled me to study it. He was my master." No man then practising at the New Hampshire bar was such a "cause-getter," and this success, as Webster was shrewd enough to see, was due quite as much to a plain and simple manner of speech as to knowledge of the law. Everything which made up what then passed for oratory was wanting. No figures of speech, no sounding sentences, no bursts of eloquence, no gestures, marred Mason's argument. In the language of the plain people, the language of the market-place and the farm, he said what he had to say and stopped. "He had a habit," said Webster, "of standing quite near the jury,—so near that he might have laid his finger on the foreman's nose,—and then he talked in a plain conversational way, in short sentences, and using no word that was not level to the comprehension of the least educated man. This led me to examine my own style, and I set about reforming it altogether."

Mr. Mason in turn has left us a description of his first encounter with Webster: "It was the first case in which he appeared at our bar; a criminal prosecution, in which I had arranged a very pretty defense, as against the attorney-general, Atkinson, who was able enough in his way, but whom I knew very well how to take. Atkinson being absent, Webster conducted the case for him, and turned in the most masterly manner the line of my defenses, carrying with him all but one of the jurors, so that I barely saved my client by my best exertions." But he saved his client, and in so doing taught Webster a lesson he was not slow to learn. Trained by such experiences, his progress from a country lawyer to a leader of the bar was rapid. The rough and overbearing manner gave place to a stately and dignified courtesy. The declamation that did so well on the Fourth of July was replaced by a style unsurpassed in modern oratory for simplicity and earnestness. The law was studied as he had never studied it before; a power was acquired of going through a mass of confusing arguments to the very heart of a question and dragging forth the vital points; and a manner of close and logical reasoning was cultivated to perfection. A few years of such application sufficed to make him a great lawyer in the community. He was retained in the leading cases, followed the Supreme Court

on its circuit, was rarely—not ten times, he says—
a junior counsel, and made, one year with another,
as much as two thousand dollars annually—a large
sum for so poor a State as New Hampshire during
the first decade of the century.

CHAPTER III

WEBSTER had now reached his first goal. Success, a good income, and some leisure were his, and having achieved this, he began to be drawn irresistibly toward politics. The profession of the law was chosen, he tells us, because his father wished it, because good friends advised it, and because the opportunity to make a fair start was then at hand. No fondness for the profession, no belief that he was specially fitted for the work, prompted him in the choice of a career.

To fish and shoot, "to contemplate nature, and to hold communion, unbroken by the presence of human beings, with this universal frame, thus wondrous fair," to read the masterpieces of Latin and English literature, to study history and government, and now and then write a paper for the "Monthly Anthology" or deliver an oration on some historic day, were far more to his liking than cross-examining witnesses and pleading before juries.

Notwithstanding this early dislike for law, Webster was long in entering on that career in which his name and fame were made, and passed his thirtieth birthday without holding a political office of any kind. He had not, however, been unmindful of what was going on about him, and had often been called on for a Fourth-of-July oration. In 1802 he spoke at Fryeburg, in 1805 at Salisbury, and in 1806 before the "Federal Gentlemen of Concord."

The Fryeburg address was not printed, but long after Webster was dead a bundle of papers found its way to an old junk-shop in Boston. The proprietor of the shop, while rummaging among the manuscripts, saw the name of Webster, and making a more careful examination, came upon the original of the Fryeburg speech, which has since been published. His theme was again the Constitution and the Union, the dangers that beset them, and the duty of guarding them. He reminded his audience that their government was free, was practical, and of their own choice. No consul dictated it; no philosophers taught its principles; it was not brought to them, as were those of Switzerland and Holland, by the bayonets of the magnanimous sister republic across the Atlantic. If they wished to preserve it they must love it, shun changes both great and small, and keep up a high tone of public morals. "When," said he, "the public mind becomes depraved, every attempt to preserve it is in vain. Laws are then nullities, and constitutions waste paper."

At Concord, as at Fryeburg, his subject was still the preservation of the Union and the spirit rather than the letter of the Constitution. Indeed, whole passages were taken from the Fryeburg oration, of which it was little more than a revision to suit the great political changes four years had wrought.

"When we speak of preserving the Constitution," said he, "we mean not the paper on which it is written, but the spirit which dwells in it. Government may lose all its real character, its genius, its temper, without losing its appearance. Republicanism, unless you guard it, will creep out of its case of parchment, like a snake out of its skin. You may have a despotism under the name of a republic. You may look on a government and see it possess all the external modes of freedom, and yet find nothing of the essence, the vitality, of freedom in it, just as you may contemplate an embalmed body, where art hath preserved proportion and form, amid nerves without motion, and veins void of blood."

It was the liberty for which the fathers fought at Lexington and Bunker Hill, the republic as they founded it, the Constitution as by them interpreted, that he believed were injured by the policy of Jefferson.

Holding these views, he went to Portsmouth, and found himself in a ship-building, ship-owning, seafaring community, whose very life depended on commerce and trade, now threatened with ruin by the edicts of Great Britain and France. The Lords Commissioners of Appeal in London had declared the broken voyage a fraud on the neutral flag, had placed more than half the commerce of America under ban, and had thrown the whole commercial world into confusion. British cruisers patrolled our coast, blockaded our ports, searched our merchantmen, impressed our seamen, attacked the *Chesapeake* on the high sea, and bore away three sailors from her deck. By an order in council, Great Britain shut to neutral trade every port of Europe from Brest to the mouth of the Elbe. Napoleon, by his Berlin decree, laid a blockade on the coast of the British Isles, commanded British property to be seized wherever found, and forbade a neutral ship that had broken the voyage by so much as touching at a British port to enter any port or colony of France. Great Britain retaliated and prohibited neutral trade between two ports both of which were in the possession of France or her allies, made the ship and cargo lawful prize when captured, and finding this of no avail, followed it with a third order more ruinous still. All the ports of France, of her allies, of their colonies, of any country at war with Great Britain, all the ports of Europe from which for any reason the British flag was barred, were shut to neutral trade save under British license. It was now the turn of Napoleon to strike again, and he did so with his Milan decree, which denationalized every ship whose captain touched at a British port, bought a British license, or submitted to search by a British officer, and made the craft the lawful prize of the captor, whether taken in a port of France or in that of one of her allies, or seized on the ocean by a man-of-war or privateer.

That our countrymen in such an emergency should have hesitated for one moment what to do, that they should have been divided in opinion, that one great party should have defended the course of Napoleon, while another with equal vehemence justified the conduct of King George, is hardly credible. But so it was, and the measures that resulted were worthy of men who carried their political differences beyond low water. Fight for the rights of neutrals and the freedom of the sea they would not; strike back so vigorously as to wound France and Great Britain they could not; but to submit with meekness they were ashamed. At least a show of resistance must be made, and in the vain hope of punishing the powers and avoiding the consequences of the decree and the orders in council, the sea was abandoned, the embargo was laid, and our countrymen adopted, in the language of the time, a terrapin policy and withdrew into their shell.

Of all the acts six-and-fifty Congresses have placed on the statute-books, the most harmful were the embargo law of 1807 and its many supplements. The first shut our ports for an unlimited time and stopped our foreign trade. The second exacted

DANIEL WEBSTER AS A YOUNG MAN.

heavy bonds from those engaged in the coasting-trade. The third spread the embargo over every harbor, lake, bay, sound, and river; exacted bonds from the owners of market-boats and oyster-boats, from the broadhorns that went down the Mississippi, and the craft that pleasure-parties used for a day's fishing; forbade export by land, and subjected every cart, wagon, wheeled vehicle, and sleigh so engaged to forfeiture, and their owners to enormous fines. The fourth prescribed that no coaster should have a clearance unless the loading was done in the presence of a revenue officer, nor sail for a port of the United States near a foreign possession without permission of the President, nor go anywhere if a collector thought fit to refuse consent. The fifth and worst of all was the Force Act. A restriction on commerce, originally intended to distress Great Britain and France, had now become perverted into an instrument for the destruction of the domestic trade and commerce of the United States, and was fast doing its work. All New England rose in resistance. Never within the memory of men then living had the people been more aroused. As a measure of coercion the embargo was declared to be a failure; as a commercial restriction it was held to be unnecessary and ruinous; as a law, the act to enforce it was claimed to be oppressive, tyrannical, and unconstitutional, and its repeal was demanded.

As Webster beheld the idle seamen, the disman-

tled ships, the grass growing on the wharves, the
closed warehouses, and the ruined merchants, he
too began to share the just indignation of the community, and, taking up his pen, wrote a Federalist pamphlet entitled "Considerations on the Embargo." No name was attached, and it was soon
lost to sight in the mass of petitions, memorials,
addresses, and resolutions that poured forth from a
score of towns and legislatures. The repeal of the
embargo laws and the press of professional work
now turned him for a time from politics; but his
interest had been aroused, hostility to the policy of
the administration had been awakened, and when
at last the war opened, he at once took the place
of opposition leader and began his political career
in earnest.

The Washington Benevolent Society of Portsmouth had invited him to deliver an oration on the
Fourth of July, 1812. Before the day came Congress had declared that a state of war existed with
Great Britain, and all New England was again
aflame with resistance. As the news passed from
one seaport to another, bells were tolled, shops
were shut, business was suspended, and the flags
on the embargoed shipping were raised to half-
mast. The sea-power of Great Britain, the weakness of the United States, the needlessness of the
war, the prospect of an alliance with Napoleon,
the wisdom of the advice of Washington, the hostility of the Republicans to New England and the

navy, the folly of intrusting the defense of the
coast to a fleet of Jefferson gunboats, and the duty
of carrying resistance to the verge of rebellion,
were the issues of the hour, and were made topics
of the speech. Hitherto the orations of Webster
on Independence Day, good as they were, contained
little more than the sentiments and historical allusions suitable to that anniversary. Now the crisis
furnished a theme deeply interesting to his audience and to himself, and, rising to the occasion, he
delivered a speech which was heard with delight,
was printed, went quickly through two editions in
pamphlet form, and greatly added to his local reputation. Two passages in particular were read with
hearty approval—that in which he condemned the
foreign policy of Jefferson, and that in which he
marked out the proper course of opposition.

Opposition of Webster's sort was, however, too
calm and reasonable to be acceptable to everybody.
The belief was wide-spread that the administration
was bent on the destruction of commerce, that it
longed for nothing so much as the ruin of New
England, that its measures were animated by a
fierce, implacable hatred of old England. Feeling
ran high, party spirit was bitter, and in a little
while notices appeared in the public journals calling on all who loved the memory of Washington
to attend a convention at Brentwood to consider
the state of the Union. Brentwood was a small
town in Rockingham County, some twenty miles

from Portsmouth, and thither Webster went.
Never before had such a gathering been known.
Men came by scores in carriages and on horseback,
till five hundred vehicles of all sorts, twice as
many horses, and two thousand men were gathered
in and about the town. To assemble in the meet-
ing-house was impossible, so a rough stage was
hastily put up out of doors, a moderator was
chosen, and stirring speeches were made by several men well known as popular orators. What
Webster said on this occasion has not been preserved, but one who was present declares that he
surpassed himself, that he surprised those who
knew his power and expected much, and that he
held the great throng spellbound for more than
ninety minutes. When the speaking was finished
a committee of seventeen, of which Webster was
one, was instructed to frame resolutions and write
a report expressive of the sense of the meeting,
while a recess of two hours was taken.

To draft so important a document in so short a
time would have been a physical impossibility.
But long before the day of meeting Webster had
been selected to prepare the report, and had
brought with him a most carefully written paper.
As he was far more used to making arguments and
delivering orations than to writing addresses, he
seems to have fancied himself the spokesman of
the convention, and put his report in the form of
an oration addressed to President Madison. He

reviewed the course of events leading up to the war, explained and justified the opposition of the Federalists of New England, urged a vigorous naval defense, and warned the President of the dangers of an alliance with Napoleon, and of the breaking up of the Union which might follow a steady adherence to the present policy. He said:

"We are, sir, from principle and habit, attached to the Union of the States. But our attachment is to the substance, and not to the form. It is to the good which this Union is capable of providing, and not to the evil which is suffered unnaturally to grow out of it. If the time should ever arrive when this Union shall be holden together by nothing but the authority of the law; when its incorporating, vital principle shall become extinct; when its principal exercises shall consist in acts of power and authority, not of protection and beneficence; when it shall lose the strong bond which it hath hitherto had in the public affections; and when, consequently, we shall be one, not in interest and mutual regard, but in name and form only—we, sir, shall look on that hour as the closing scene of our country's prosperity.

"We shrink from the separation of these States as an event fraught with incalculable evils, and it is among our strongest objections to the present course of measures that they have, in our opinion, a very dangerous and alarming bearing on such an event. If a separation of the States ever should

4

take place, it will be on some occasion when one portion of the country undertakes to control, to regulate, and to sacrifice the interests of another, when a small and heated majority in the government, taking counsel of their passions and not of their reason, contemptuously disregarding the interests and perhaps stopping the mouths of a large and respectable minority, shall, by hasty, rash, and ruinous measures, threaten to destroy essential rights and lay waste the most important interests.

"It shall be our most fervent supplication to Heaven to avert both the event and the occasion, and the government may be assured that the tie which binds us to the Union will never be broken by us."

The resolutions and the address to the President having been adopted, the convention proceeded to nominate men to represent New Hampshire in the Thirteenth Congress. The custom of dividing the State into as many districts as it had members of the House of Representatives, and assigning to the voters in each the duty of electing one, had not then come into use. Each party named six candidates, and the general ticket so framed was voted for all over the State. Among the six names on the Federalist ticket now prepared at Brentwood was that of Webster, and when the election came off it stood at the head of the poll. He received two more votes than any other Federalist and twenty-five hundred more than any of the six Republicans. He was now a member of Congress. He had reached the goal for which his father longed, and as he heard the result of the hotly contested canvass, his thoughts must have gone back to that day in the hay-field when the stern old soldier told him of a disappointed ambition and implored him to "learn, learn," that he might not be doomed to that life of toil which had made his father old before his time.

CHAPTER IV

A CONGRESSMAN FROM NEW HAMPSHIRE

WHEN Webster reached Washington in the month of May, 1813, and took his seat in the House of Representatives, his career as a politician began. Never before had he filled any political office, elective or appointive. He came with no reputation earned by service of a public sort. Not a member of the House, in all likelihood, had ever read one of his Fourth-of-July orations, or had ever heard him argue a case, or, unless from New England, had ever heard his name. Yet the striking presence of the man attracted notice, and when Speaker Clay was forming the committees, he chose Webster to be the one representative of the Federalists on the Committee on Foreign Relations. At the head of that committee was Calhoun. The entrance of Webster into Congress, therefore, completed the great triumvirate of American politics, and the three men whose names thenceforth for forty years are never absent from our annals met for the first time.

As one of the minority party, Webster's duties for a while lay easy upon him. He was responsible for nothing but reasonable opposition, and while waiting for something to oppose, spent his days mingling with the strange society of the capital. "I went yesterday to make my bow to the President. I do not like his looks any better than I like his administration. I think I could find clearly in his features embargo, non-intercourse, and war. Dawson and Findlay are the makers of all motions. Findlay makes his from the journal of the last session, which he holds in his hands and reads. Dawson is as inspired an animal as one could wish to see."

Nothing seemed to Webster more noticeable than the absence of women; for few congressmen could then afford to bring their families to Washington and there maintain them on six dollars a day. "A few ladies," says he, "are to be seen by going to the weekly rout at the palace; but they are there only as so many curiosities, *rarae aves*, fit for all the purposes of social life save only the unimportant particulars of speaking and being spoken to. I understand that in the winter session, when there are more ladies in the city, the aforesaid evil is in some degree mitigated. I have been to the levee, or drawing-room, but once. It is a mere matter of form. You make your bow to Mrs. Madison, and to Mr. Madison if he comes in your way; but he, being there merely as a guest, is not officially entitled to your congé. M. Serurier, Mme. Bonaparte, the Russian minister, heads of departments and tails of departments, members of Congress, etc., etc., here and there interspersed with military and naval hat and coat, make up the group. You stay from five minutes to an hour, as you please, eat and drink what you can catch without danger of surfeit, and if you can luckily find your hat and stick, then take French leave; and that 's going to the 'levee.' "

But it was not in search of social pleasure that Webster went to Washington. The Congress had been called in extra session to find a way to help the government out of the straits into which a long series of military and financial disasters had brought it. Those splendid sea victories which make the years 1812 and 1813 glorious in our history were still of constant occurrence. But the war on land had failed miserably. The conquest of Canada, so boldly predicted, had not been achieved. Hull had surrendered one army at Detroit. Another still lingered on the banks of the Niagara. A third, sent to attack Montreal, was in winter quarters in New York.

The loan on which the administration depended for means with which to carry on the war, after being twice rejected by the people, had been sold to a syndicate at a heavy discount. The coast from Point Judith to the Mississippi River was closely blockaded, and New England was in a state of angry resistance which bordered on rebellion.

As a member of a New England delegation, it

was now the duty of Webster to carry opposition to the war and the administration from the town-meeting to the floor of the House of Representatives. In just what that opposition should consist, had been stated by him in a speech before the Washington Benevolent Society at Portsmouth on the Fourth of July, 1812:

"Resistance and insurrection form no part of our creed. The disciples of Washington are neither tyrants in power nor rebels out. If we are taxed to carry on this war, we shall disregard certain distinguished examples, and shall pay. If our personal services are required, we shall yield them to the precise extent of our constitutional liability. At the same time the world may be assured that we know our rights and shall exercise them. We shall express our opinions on this, as on every measure of government, I trust, without passion; I am certain, without fear.

"We believe, then, that this war is not the result of impartial policy. If there be cause of war against England, there is still more abundant cause of war against France. The war is professedly undertaken principally on account of the continuance of the British orders in council. It is well known that those orders, odious as they are, did not begin the unjust and vexatious system practised upon neutrals, nor would that system end with those orders if we should obtain the object of the war by procuring their repeal. The decrees of

France are earlier in point of time, more extravagant in their pretensions, and tenfold more injurious in their consequences. They are aggravated by a pretended abrogation, and, holding our understandings in no higher estimation than our rights, that nation requires us to believe in the repeal of edicts the daily operation of which is manifest and visible before our eyes.''

Having thus declared himself in favor of a bold criticism of the conduct of the administration, and having been elected by the votes of men bitterly opposed to the war as unnecessary, partial, and unjust, it would never do to go back to Portsmouth without at least one blow against ''Mr. Madison's war.'' That he should strike such a blow was all the more necessary because the opposition in the House was unorganized and unled. There was no well-defined plan of action; no ''steering committee'' to see that a plan, if formed, was carried out; no one man on the floor who stood in the same relation to the Federalists that Calhoun did to the Republicans. In this state of affairs Webster chose to act for himself, and before he had been three weeks in the House, he offered a set of resolutions which brought him at once into public notice.

The long embargo, having failed to compel either power to remove its restrictions on neutral commerce, had been replaced, in March, 1809, by the non-intercourse act, which had been enforced as to France and suspended as to Great Britain by agreement with her minister. But the act of the minister had been promptly disavowed by Great Britain, and non-intercourse restored, while Napoleon struck back with the secret decree of Vienna, which never was published, but sequestered every ship that came to any port within Napoleon's power.

The non-intercourse act of 1809, having failed, as did the embargo, to produce the wished-for effect on France and Great Britain, was repealed in 1810 and replaced by Macon bill No. 2, which restored commercial relations with all the world, but bade the President, "in case either Great Britain or France shall, before the 3d day of March next [1811], so revoke or modify her edicts as that they shall cease to violate the neutral commerce of the United States," to forbid intercourse with the nation which had not revoked its edicts. Quick to see the advantage afforded, Napoleon declared, through his minister Cadore (August 5, 1810), that the decrees of Berlin and Milan were repealed, and would cease to have effect after November 1, provided Great Britain revoked her orders in council or the United States should "cause their rights to be respected by the English." Accepting this statement as proof of repeal, Madison, on November 2, issued a proclamation announcing the fact, and the Secretary of the Treasury informed the collectors of customs that three months from that day (on February 2, 1811) commercial intercourse with Great Britain would end, unless the orders in council should be recalled before the expiration of the three months' period. But Great Britain denied that the Berlin and Milan decrees were repealed, refused to recall or modify the orders in council, and the war followed.

In their attacks on the administration the Federalists took the ground that if war had to come it should have been made against France as well as Great Britain; that she was the first to attack neutrals; that she was still their enemy; that the Berlin and Milan decrees had never been repealed, and in proof of this pointed to the speech of Napoleon in March, 1811, to the deputies from the Hanseatic League, plainly stating that "the decrees of Berlin and Milan are the fundamental laws of my empire," and to decisions of the French courts of admiralty. The Republicans in reply declared that war on France would be infamous; that her decrees were not in force; and pointed to other decisions of the French admiralty courts and to a letter of M. Champagny, Minister of Foreign Affairs, asserting that the decrees had been revoked.

In the midst of this angry dispute, the President laid before Congress a document that made matters worse than before. It was a letter from the American minister at Paris stating that one day in May, 1812, the Duke of Bassano had assured him that the Berlin and Milan decrees had been revoked as far back as April, 1811; that their revoca-

tion had been announced to our then minister; and
that a copy of the repealing decree had been sent
to the French minister at Washington for delivery
to the Secretary of State. If this were so, then
Madison, the Federalists claimed, had suppressed
the information; had furnished Great Britain with
her only pretext for refusing to recall the orders
in council; had suffered his country to enter on
a war ruinous to trade; and was responsible for all
the distress, all the expense, and all the blood that
had been or might be shed. The Republicans entered a flat denial to all this, and did not hesitate
to say that Bassano had lied. The question thus
turned on the veracity of the duke, and a demand
was made "that the subject be brought into notice
at the approaching session of Congress, and that
measures be taken which will at least force the
President to say whether the declaration of Bassano to Mr. Barlow is true or false."

Seizing on this as a good ground from which
to attack the administration, Webster made it the
subject of his resolutions of inquiry. He called
on the President to inform the House when, by
whom, and in what manner the repeal of the French
decrees was first made known to the government;
whether Mr. Russell, the late chargé of the United
States at Paris, had ever admitted or denied the
truth of the statement of the Duke of Bassano;
whether the French minister at Washington ever
informed the government of the repeal of the de-

crees; and, in case the first information was that communicated to Mr. Barlow by the Duke of Bassano in 1812, whether the government had ever required of France any explanation why the repealing decree had so long been concealed, and if such explanation had been given, whether it had been followed by a remonstrance.

The debate which now arose ran on for four days, greatly excited the House, drew large crowds, and was still at its height when the opposition gave way, and each resolution was carried by a handsome majority.

Webster's story of what happened during the four days is told in a series of daily letters to his friend March, in New York. "The resolutions," which he forwards to Mr. March, with a request to insert them in the "Commercial Advertiser" and send copies to certain gentlemen he names, "were offered yesterday. What the House will do with them I cannot say. The question to consider was carried—one hundred and thirty-two to twenty-eight. I have done what I thought my duty. I am easy about the result." "Mr. Bibb asked me not to call up my resolutions till to-morrow. He said he was willing to vote for the four first. Whether he really so intends I cannot say. If the party wishes to oppose them and give us battle, so be it. If any fault is found with my resolutions in your city, let me know it."

"The resolutions have passed, unaltered except-

THE CAPITOL, 1814.   FROM A DRAWING IN THE CONGRESSIONAL LIBRARY.

ing the usual saving clause in the last resolution, which was left out by accident. I made no speech. When I came to the House this morning, Calhoun told me the motion for indefinite postponement would be withdrawn, his motion to amend withdrawn, and he and some of his friends should vote for these resolutions as they are. I, of course, could not object. They have acted very strangely. A dozen motions made and withdrawn—some pulling one way, some another. They do not manage like so many Solomons.''

''No one,'' said a newspaper of the day, ''who hurried to the House yesterday morning expected an abandonment of all opposition on the part of the majority. But such was the fact. Many of the leaders of the Republican party voted for the resolution. This singular and unexpected compromise, after a debate that promised to excite not a little asperity, has puzzled every one not informed of the reasons which induced the majority to concede the information. We think it highly probable that the President has been consulted on the subject and has advised the observance of the course ultimately adopted.'' The resolutions having been approved by the House, Webster and a fellow-member were sent with them to the White House, or, to use his own words, ''Mr. Rhea, after my resolutions passed, made a little resolution calling for information on the Prince Regent's Declaration—passed. The Speaker has appointed me and

old Rhea to carry the resolutions to the palace!!—
I never swear.''

"You have learned the fate of my resolutions,"
Webster wrote to his brother. "We had a warm
time of it for four days, and then the other side
declined further discussion. I had prepared myself for a little speech, but the necessity of speaking was prevented. I went with Rhea of Tennessee
to deliver the resolutions to the President. I found
him in bed, sick of a fever. I gave them to him,
and he merely answered that they would be attended to. We have received no answer.'' In another letter he draws a more graphic picture: "I
went on Tuesday to the palace to present the resolutions. The President was in his bed, sick of a
fever, his nightcap on his head, his wife attending
him. I think he will find no relief from my pre-
scription. . . . How will Madison answer the
part of [the] resolutions calling for his correspondence with Serurier? In truth, there never was a
party acted so awkwardly as the Demos did through
the whole of that business.'' But "he will be followed up on that subject. An inquiry into the
failure on the frontier is talked of; I think there
will not be any time this session. We have several projects, and a good many good hands to give
a lift. We are trying to organize our opposition
and bring all our forces to act in concert. There
is recently appointed a kind of committee to super-
intend our concerns.'' Of this Webster was a mem-

ber. A career of six weeks in the House had made him a leader of his party and brought him reputation as a speaker. One who was present when the resolutions were offered asserts that no member "ever riveted the attention of the House so completely in his first speech"; that "members left their seats and came out on the floor that they might see him face to face; listened attentively, and when he finished, went up and warmly congratulated the orator." But a better testimonial as to the effect of that maiden speech is furnished by Chief Justice Marshall. Nearly twenty years later, when the name of Webster was known over all the land, a copy of his "Speeches and Forensic Arguments" was sent to the great judge, who went straightway to Justice Story, and expressed his regret that two were not in the collection—that on the resolutions calling for proof of the repeal of the French decrees, and another on the previous question. "I read these speeches," said Marshall, "with very great pleasure and satisfaction at the time. When the first was delivered I did not know Mr. Webster; but I was so much struck with it that I did not hesitate then to state that Mr. Webster was a very able man, and would become one of the very first statesmen in America, and perhaps the very first."

When at last the President's answer came, Webster had gone back to Portsmouth, and action was put off to the regular session. By that time the steering committee had formed a plan of opposition, and when the session was well under way, one member offered resolutions calling on the President for an account of the state of our relations with France, another for information explaining the cause of the failure of our arms along the northern frontier, and Webster for the consideration of the President's answer to his resolutions of the last session. To this the House consented so far as to make them the order for a certain day; but the discussion never took place. "They are determined," he wrote to his brother, "not to take up my resolutions this session; of this I am certain. But on the loan bill we hope to get a blow at them." His own chance "to get a blow at them" came when the bill for the encouragement of enlistments was put upon its passage. While the details of the bill were under debate he said nothing; but when it had been read the third time he could contain himself no longer, and hastily putting together an outline of what he would say, delivered the first of his many celebrated speeches.

"I inclose you," he wrote to Ezekiel, "a few creatures called speeches. One of them you will find I have corrected, in some of its printer's errors, with my pen. Please do the same with the rest before they go out of your hands. I shall send a few to your townsmen; you will learn who by looking at the post-office, for I have not my list by me now, and so cannot say exactly for whom I shall send to you. Of those that come to your hands give them in my name to those you think proper, Federalists or Democrats.

"The speech is not exactly what it ought to be; I had not time. I had no intention of speaking till nine o'clock in the morning, and delivered the thing about two. I could make it better, but I dare say you think it would be easier to make a new one than to mend it. It was well enough received at the time, and our side of the House said they would have it in this form. So much for speeches."

"The thing," as he states, was hastily put together; but it had little to do with the questions under debate and much with the policy of the administration. All the pent-up opposition which had been rankling in his breast since he first took his seat in the House now found an outlet. The speech was really delivered to his constituents, was at best only a good campaign document, and, before election day came around, was used as such. But when he next addressed the House his subject was more serious, and he had something to say on a question soon to become a living issue.

The President, in a special message to the House, had asked for an embargo. Our coast from Rhode Island southward was then in a state of rigorous blockade; but New England was not molested, and into her ports came British ships disguised as neutrals and loaded with such goods as found a ready

5

market in the South. These, loaded on wagons, were carried as far as Charleston and Augusta. But the raw cotton the wagons brought back to Newburyport and Boston was less in value than the manufactured wares they took to the Carolinas and Georgia, and a heavy balance remained to be settled in specie. To stop this trade, prevent the export of gold and silver, inflict on the seaports of New England the same hardships the blockade imposed elsewhere, and cut off the supply of food passing the boundary into Canada, was the object of Madison's request. With it Congress at once complied, and the first act of the session was another embargo law. But scarcely was it in force when a vessel arrived at Annapolis with the offer of Castlereagh to negotiate for peace, and with newspapers describing the defeat at Leipsic. Napoleon was now overthrown; the armies of the Allies had crossed the Rhine; Holland was given her old-time boundary; and all decrees and orders in council were things of the past. To keep up an embargo was madness, and in March, 1814, Madison asked for its repeal. The message was hailed by all Federalists with delight, and when the bill repealing the whole restrictive system was before the House, Webster gave expression to his feelings in joyous terms.

"I am happy to be present at the office now to be performed, and to act a part in the funeral ceremonies of what has been called the restrictive system. The occasion, I think, will justify a temperate and moderate exultation on the part of those who have constantly opposed this system of politics and uniformly foretold its miserable end. I congratulate my friends on the triumph of their principles. At the same time, I would not refuse condolence to the few surviving friends to whose affections th~ deceased was precious, who are overwhelmed with affliction at its sudden dissolution, and who sorrow most of all that they shall see its face no more. The system, sir, which we are now about to explode, is likely to make no inconsiderable figure in our history. It was originally offered to the people of this country as a kind of political faith. It was to be believed, not examined. They were to act upon, not reason about, it. No saint in the calendar ever had a set of followers less at liberty or less disposed to indulge troublesome inquiry than some, at least, of those on whom this system depended for support. Yet, notwithstanding all this, in a moment, in the twinkling of an eye, the whole system is dissolved. The embargo act, the non-importation act, and all the crowd of additions and supplements, together with all their garniture of messages, reports, and resolutions, are tumbling undistinguished into one common grave. But yesterday this policy had a thousand friends and supporters; to-day it is fallen and prostrate, and few 'so poor to do it reverence.'

"Sir, a government which cannot administer the

affairs of a nation without producing so frequent and such violent alterations in the ordinary occupations and pursuits of private life has, in my opinion, little claim to the regard of this community. It has been said that the system of commercial restrictions was favorable to domestic manufactures, and that if it did nothing but induce the habit of providing for our own wants by our own means, it would deserve to be esteemed a blessing. Something is, indeed, said in the message in relation to the continuance of the double duties 'as a more effectual safeguard and encouragement to our growing manufactures.' Sir, I consider the imposition of double duties as a mere financial measure. Its great object was to raise revenue, not to foster manufactures. In respect to manufactures it is necessary to speak with some precision.

"I am not, generally speaking, their enemy; I am their friend: but I am not for rearing them, or any other interest, in hotbeds. I would not legislate precipitately, even in favor of them. I feel no desire to push capital into extensive manufactures faster than the general progress of our wealth and population propels it. I am not in haste to see Sheffields and Birminghams in America. Until the population of the country shall be greater in proportion to its extent, such establishments would be impracticable if attempted, and if practicable, they would be unwise. I am not anxious to accelerate the approach of the period when the great mass of American labor shall not find its employment in the field; when the young men of the country shall be obliged to shut their eyes upon external nature, upon the heavens and the earth, and immerse themselves in close and unwholesome workshops; when they shall be obliged to shut their ears to the bleating of their own flocks upon their own hills, and to the voice of the lark that cheers them at their plows, that they may open them in dust and smoke and steam to the perpetual whirl of spools and spindles, and the grating of rasps and saws.

"It is the true policy of government to suffer the different pursuits of society to take their own course, and not to give excessive bounties or encouragements to one over another. This also is the true spirit of the Constitution. It has not, in my opinion, conferred on the government this power of changing the occupations of the people."

Opposition to the policy of the administration was Webster's guiding principle. Neither at this nor during the next session of Congress did he introduce any bill or support any measure of real importance to his countrymen. He was simply a Federalist, bound to embarrass the President at every turn, though the enemy's fleets were blockading the ports and the enemy's troops were actually in possession of a portion of the soil of his country. How far he was willing to carry this resistance is well set forth by his vote against the tax bill at the following session.

The government was then hard put. During

the summer of 1814 a British fleet had come up
the Chesapeake Bay, and a force of the enemy had
marched inland and burned the Capitol, the "palace," and some public buildings. The State banks
outside of New England had suspended specie payment, and the federal treasury, unable to use its
funds, was on the verge of bankruptcy. All Maine
east of the Penobscot River was in British hands,
and had been formally declared British territory;
and it was well known that an expedition against
New Orleans was under way.

In our day the man who, in such a crisis, thinking only of his party, should forget his country
and seek to withhold the means needed to rescue
it from the dangers that pressed on every side,
would merit and receive the execrations of all
right-minded persons. It was not so, however, in
the time of Madison, and when the Republicans
asked for a national bank, a conscript law, and
more taxes, the Federalists had nothing but ridi-
cule and opposition to offer. To a bank, if required to redeem its notes at all times in specie,
Webster had no objection; but he gave his vote
against every form of bank the Republicans submitted, "had a hand," as he expressed it, "in overthrowing Mr. Monroe's conscription," and voted
against the taxes.

As yet no really patriotic sentiment seems to
animate him. No word of encouragement escapes
his lips. He will support the war if fought on the

ocean; he will express his opinion on the conduct
of the war as freely and boldly as he pleases; but
he will not do anything which can be twisted into
approval or support of the administration. Nor
do his letters during this period show any opinion
of his own as to the true public policy. On the
other hand, he is rather pleased as the difficulties
become greater. "Poor Madison does not know
what to do"; "Never was more sinking fortune";
"Poor Madison, I doubt whether he has had a
night's sleep these three weeks"; "The taxes go
heavily; I fear they will not go at all. They are in
a great pickle. Who cares?" are the sort of expressions with which his correspondence abounds.

Webster had now finished his first term as a
member of the House, and was easily reëlected to a
second. But the place seems to have lost its charm.
The pay was small, the duties were great, while
his need of a larger income and time to earn it was
imperative. "You must contrive some way for
me to get rich as soon as there is peace," he writes.
The great fire at Portsmouth in December, 1813,
which burned two hundred and forty buildings and
laid bare a tract fifteen acres in extent, had destroyed his house and library, and inflicted a loss
of some six thousand dollars. The savings of years
were swept away and must be made good again.
To attempt this in Portsmouth, where, at most,
only a couple of thousands could be gathered each
year, when the same industry applied elsewhere

would yield richer returns, seemed unwise. But where should the new hazard be made? Many inducements drew him to Boston, and as the session of 1815–16 wore away, he began to think of abandoning New England and settling in Albany or New York, and in March wrote to Ezekiel: "I have settled my purpose to remove from New Hampshire in the course of the summer. I have thought of Boston, New York, and Albany. On the whole, I shall probably go to Boston, although I am not without some inducement to go into the State of New York. Our New England prosperity and importance are passing away. This is fact. The events of the times, the policy of England, the consequences of our war, and the treaty of Ghent, have bereft us of our commerce, the great source of our wealth. If any great scenes are to be acted in this country within the next twenty years, New York is the place in which those scenes are to be viewed."

Yet, in spite of the fair prospects of New York, he chose Boston, moved thither in the summer of 1816, and thenceforth remained a citizen of Massachusetts. Removal to Boston cost him his seat in Congress. But it mattered little, as he could not, in all probability, have been reëlected, for, in common with eighty other congressmen, he had voted for the compensation bill.

Since the establishment of government under the Constitution the pay of congressmen had been six

WEBSTER'S HOUSE IN
SOMERSET STREET, BOSTON.

SEAL.

WEBSTER'S CHAIR
AND STICK.

dollars for each day they attended, and mileage from and to their homes. But, in the course of a quarter-century, salaries had gone up, the cost of living had greatly increased, and members who had not other sources of income found it impossible to live as they wished on what had become low wages. With many misgivings and explanations, the daily allowance was therefore changed to a salary of fifteen hundred dollars a year. Some grumbling and fault-finding was expected. But when constituents, grand juries, legislatures, public meetings, and the press from Maine to Louisiana joined in one universal denunciation of every man who voted aye, the situation became serious. Nine members of the House during the summer of 1816 resigned in disgust, and refused to serve out their terms. Scores of others were not renominated, and in the autumn elections State after State changed its representation completely, or sent back such members only as had opposed the law. Not one of the old members was returned from Ohio, Delaware, and Vermont. Half the New Hampshire delegation was retired; all but one of the Georgians; five out of nine Marylanders; ten out of twenty-three Pennsylvanians; six out of nine South-Carolinians. Five out of seven members from Connecticut were not even renominated. That the people should grow angry over a matter so clearly for the public good, yet remain heedless of others that injured them much, disgusted Webster, and brought on one of the fits of political hopelessness from which he often suffered.

"We are doing nothing now," he wrote in January, 1817, "but to quarrel with one of our laws of last session, called the horse law, its object being to pay the Kentucky men for all the horses which died in that country during the war. So far very well; but there was a clause put in to pay for all houses and buildings burned by the enemy on account of having been a military depot. This played the very d——. All the Niagara frontier, the city of Washington, etc., wherever the enemy destroyed anything, was proved to have been a military depot: one tavern, twenty-seven thousand dollars, because some officers or soldiers lodged in the house a day or two before the burning; one great rope-walk, because a rope had been sent there to be mended for the navy-yard; etc.

"We then have the compensation [bill] to repeal, which I trust will not take us long. Then comes from the Senate the 'conscription law,' as you justly call it. What inducement has one to resist this or anything else? Two years ago, with infinite pains and labor, we defeated Mr. Monroe's conscription. Nobody thanked us for it. Last winter our friends in the Senate got this militia bill thrown out; nobody knew or cared anything about it. For two or three years Massachusetts has been paying from ten to twenty-five per cent. more duties on importations than Pennsylvania or Maryland.

At the close of last session we tried to do something for her relief; but her federal legislature takes no notice of the abominable injustice done her, or the plain violations of the Constitution and the laws which have taken place to her great injury. All are silent and quiet. But when her federal members, who come here to be kicked and stoned and abused in her behalf, think proper to raise their compensation so that it will defray their expenses, she denounces them man by man without an exception. No respect for talents, services, character, or feelings restrains her from joining with the lowest democracy in its loudest cry.''

CHAPTER V

THE next five years of his life were spent in the practice of law in the courts of Massachusetts and before the Supreme Court of the United States. The times were bad. Never had the country known a period of such severe and wide-spread business depression. Years afterward, men who remembered those days still spoke of them as the "hard times of eighteen hundred and starve to death." Yet, in spite of this, the account-books of Webster show that during the worst year of all he received fifteen thousand dollars in fees. But the gain in fame was greater than in money, for then was it that he won the Dartmouth College case, delivered the great speech at Plymouth, and achieved distinction in the convention called to amend the Constitution of Massachusetts. "Our friend Webster," said Judge Story, "has gained a noble reputation. It was a glorious field for him, and he had an ample harvest. The whole force of his great mind was brought out, and in several speeches he commanded universal admiration." It was indeed a glorious field for him. For twenty years he had been studying what he well called "the nature and constitution of society and government in this country," and now, for the first time, found an occasion to state his opinions at length. The speech on the judiciary, that on religion as a qualification for office-holding, and, above all, that on property as the basis of representation in the Senate, were much admired, and carried conviction to his listeners. Of this last he was not a little proud, and five days after the delivery of it in the convention he repeated it, word for word, to the crowd that gathered in the little church at Plymouth, as part of the oration on "The First Settlement of New England."

With each increase of fame as a lawyer and an orator, friends and admirers grew more and more urgent that he should once more return to public life. He did, indeed, consent to serve as a Presidential elector, and for ten days sat in the Massachusetts legislature. Many years afterward, in the course of a speech, Webster referred to this service, and told his hearers a story quite characteristic of the man. "It so happens," said he, "that all the public services which I have rendered in this world, in my day and generation, have been connected with the general government. I think I ought to make one exception. I was ten days a member of the Massachusetts legislature, and I turned my thoughts to the search for some good object in which I could be useful in that position; and, after

much reflection, I introduced a bill which, with the
general consent of both houses of the Massachusetts legislature, passed into a law, and is now a
law of the State, which enacts that no man in the
State shall catch trout in any other manner than
in the old way, with an ordinary hook and line.''

To keep aloof from public life, however, was
not possible. To the end of his life Webster was,
above all else, a student and an expounder of constitutional government, and the period we have now
reached was one in which those principles were
everywhere discussed. In the Supreme Court,
Marshall was handing down one by one decisions
upholding the jurisdiction of the court, defining
the powers of Congress, limiting the powers of the
States, and completely changing the popular understanding of the place of the judiciary in our
system of government. All about him new State
constitutions were being made and old ones
mended. Within the brief period of five years, In-
diana, Illinois, Alabama, Mississippi, Connecticut,
Maine, and Missouri had each framed a new instrument of government, and New York, Massachusetts, and Maryland had greatly changed their
early forms. The extension of the franchise, the
basis of representation, the qualifications for office-holding, were everywhere discussed. Eco-
nomic and industrial issues had come to the front
and were pressing for settlement. The right of
Congress to protect manufactures, to charter a na-

tional bank, to build roads and canals, to prohibit
slavery in a new State, were topics to which Webster could not be indifferent.

A great opportunity now lay before him, and
when, one day in August, 1822, a committee from a
meeting of delegates from all the wards of Boston
invited him to represent the district of Suffolk in
Congress, he consented, and in December, 1823,
was again a member of the House.

The spirit in which he entered on the new service
is finely set forth in a letter to Judge Story, written in May, 1823: "I never felt more down sick on
all subjects connected with the public than at the
present moment. I have heretofore cherished a
faint hope that New England would some time or
other get out of this miserable, dirty squabble of
local politics, and assert her proper character and
consequence. But I at length give up. I feel the
hand of fate upon us, and to struggle is in vain.
We are doomed to be hewers of wood and drawers
of water, and I am prepared henceforth to do my
part of the drudgery without hoping for an end.
What has sickened me beyond remedy is the tone
and temper of these disputes. We are disgraced
beyond help or hope by these things. There is a
Federal interest, a Democratic interest, a bankrupt
interest, an orthodox interest, and a middling interest; but I see no national interest, nor any national feeling in the whole matter."

Happily, he was not prepared to do his part of

the drudgery without hoping for an end. So far as he was concerned, the end had come. The "miserable squabble of local politics," which so strongly affected his conduct during his first term of service in the House, was to influence him no more. At last he had risen to the plane of statesmanship, and was to see the coming issues in their bearings on the nation.

As the autumn wore away, and the time drew near when Congress was to meet, he began, in his usual way, to turn over in his mind what he should do. As a student of constitutional government and a lover of liberty, the unhappy failure of the republican movement in South America, the sudden rise of liberalism in Europe, the stamping out of every trace of democracy by the Holy Allies at Naples and in Spain, and the glorious struggle of the Greeks for independence, interested him deeply. The cause of the Greeks, and their appeal to the one real republic of the world, touched him.

"If nobody does it who can do it better," he wrote in November to his friend Everett, "I shall certainly say something of the Greeks. The miserable issue of the Spanish revolution makes the Greek cause more interesting, and I begin to think they have character enough to carry them through the contest with success." This purpose grew stronger the more he thought it over, and when, on reaching New York, he took up the October number of the "North American Review" and read Mr. Everett's article on the Greeks, he firmly resolved to help them. "I have found leisure here," he wrote, "and not till now, to read your admirable article on the Greeks. Since I left Boston, also, we have had important information from them. I feel a great inclination to say or do something in their behalf early in the session, if I know what to say or to do. If you can readily direct me to any source from which I can obtain more information than is already public respecting these affairs, I would be obliged to you to do so."

Mr. Everett having responded in the most handsome manner, sent him manuscripts and bits of information, and posted him in all the details of the war, Webster wrote to him: "I have gone over your two manuscripts with the map before me, and think I have mastered the campaigns of 1821–22 historically and topographically. My wonder is, where and how your most extraordinary industry has been able to find all the materials for so interesting and detailed a narrative. I hope you will send me a digested narrative of the events of this year so far as they are to be learned from the last accounts.

"I have spoken to several gentlemen on the subject of a motion respecting Greece, and all of them approve it. The object which I wish to bring about, and which I believe may be brought about, is the appointment of a commissioner to go to

Greece. Two modes present themselves. A motion to that effect and a speech in support of it, giving some account of the rise and progress of the Greek revolution, and showing the propriety and utility of the proposed mission. The other is to raise a committee on the subject and let there be a report containing the same matter. Whichever may be adopted, your communications are invaluable, and I wish you would tell me frankly how far I can use them without injury to your January article in the 'North American.' We can wait until that article is out, if you think best, but my impression is, we should do well to bring forward the subject within ten or twelve days from this time, while the House is not yet much occupied, and while the country feels the warmth communicated by the President's message. I intend to see, in the course of this day and to-morrow, Mr. R. King, Mr. Clay, and perhaps the President, and have their views on this matter.''

But Monroe, in his message, had announced the famous doctrine that still bears his name, and was little inclined to meddle with affairs in Greece. ''There was, I believe,'' Webster continues, ''a meeting of the members of the administration yesterday, at which, *inter alia*, they talked of Greece. The pinch is that in the message the President has taken pretty high ground as to this continent, and is afraid of the appearance of interfering in the concerns of the other continent also. This does not weigh greatly with me; I think we have as much community with the Greeks as with the inhabitants of the Andes and the dwellers on the borders of the Vermilion Sea. If nothing should occur to alter my present purpose, I shall bring forward a motion on the subject on Monday, and shall propose to let it lie on the table for a fortnight."

On the day chosen Webster accordingly moved that provision ought to be made to defray the expense of sending an agent or commissioner to Greece whenever the President should deem it expedient to make an appointment. For six weeks the resolution lay on the table. During this time Webster was busy with his speech. "I believe," he wrote, "there will be a good deal of discussion, although, if any, pretty much on one side. While some of our Boston friends, as I know, think this resolution even quixotic, leading to a crusade, it will be objected to strongly by many on account of its tame milk-and-water character. The merchants are naturally enough a little afraid about their cargoes at Smyrna; besides, Greece is a great way off, etc.

"My intention is to justify the resolution against two classes of objectors, those that suppose it not to go far enough, and those that suppose it to go too far; then, to give some little history of the Greek revolution, express a pretty strong conviction of its ultimate success, and persuade the

House, if I can, to take the merit of being the first government among all civilized nations who have publicly rejoiced in the emancipation of Greece. I feel now that I could make a pretty good speech for my friends the Greeks, but I shall get cool in fourteen days, unless you keep up my temperature.''

The intent and purpose of the speech, however, were not understood. It was believed that Webster had seized on the topic because it was uppermost in the public mind, because of the feeling and wide-spread interest it had awakened, and because it would enable him to mark his return to Congress by an oration finer than that delivered in the old First Church at Plymouth. When, therefore, he rose to speak, on the day appointed to consider his resolution, and looked over the sea of eager faces drawn to the House by the expectation of a display of oratory, he felt in duty bound to say that ''he was afraid that, so far as he was concerned, the excited expectations of the public mind, on the present occasion, would be disappointed.'' But the public mind suffered no disappointment. ''The report of your speech,'' wrote Joseph Hopkinson, ''meager as it is, shows the foot of Hercules; but we want the whole body, and trust you will give it to us. Mr. Hemphill wrote me it was the best he ever heard.''

While the House admired the oratory, it would not be persuaded by the argument. Member after

JAMES MADISON.

JOHN MARSHALL.

JAMES MONROE.

member spoke in opposition. Some thought the resolution little better than a declaration of war. Others feared it would lead to war. Still others felt so sure that the Holy Allies would soon attack the South American republics, and we be called on to make good the stand taken by the President in his message, that they shrank from "mingling in the turmoils of Europe" when we might ourselves, in a little while, be struggling for the preservation of our own liberties. After a week of debating the Committee of the Whole rose without asking leave to sit again, and for a second time a resolution offered by Webster never reached a vote. "The motion," he wrote Mr. Mason, "ought to have been adopted, and would have been by a general vote but for certain reasons, which the public will never know, and which I will not trouble you with now. I could divide the House very evenly on the subject now, and perhaps carry a vote. Whether I shall stir it again must be considered. Mr. Adams' opposition to it was the most formidable obstacle." A few years later, when a writer in the "Philadelphia Quarterly" reviewed a volume of his collected speeches, Webster wrote to the reviewer and said: "One word about the Greek speech. I think I am more fond of this child than of any of the family. My object, when the resolution was introduced, was not understood. It was imagined that, seeing the existence of a warm public sympathy for the suffering Greeks, the purpose was only to make a speech responsive

and gratifying to that sympathy. The real object
was larger. It was to take occasion of the Greek
revolution, and the conduct held in regard to it
by the great Continental Powers, to exhibit the
principles laid down by those powers as the basis
on which they meant to maintain the peace of
Europe. This purpose made it necessary to examine accurately the proceedings of all the Congresses from that of Paris in 1814 to that of Laybach in 1821. I read those proceedings with a
good deal of attention, and endeavored to extract
the principle on which they were founded. There
is nothing in the book which I think so well of
as parts of this speech. Events have shown that
some opinions here expressed were well founded.
A revolution has taken place, and the people reform their constitution and then invite an individual to the throne *on condition* of governing according to the constitution. Belgium is doing the
same; Poland is attempting to do the same. This
is the spirit of the English Revolution of 1688, but
it is flat burglary according to the law of Laybach.

"I was something of a prophet, too, in regard
to the duration of the French monarchy. See Plymouth Discourse. But enough; I am tired of saying 'I,' 'me,' 'mine.' My dear sir, if the world
cannot see the merit of my illustrious works, why
should I (or why should you) trouble ourselves
to point them out?"[1]

[1] Curtis's Life of Webster.

The speech was indeed a great one, was always held by Webster to be his best, and was prepared with much pains and labor. His rough notes, still preserved in the New Hampshire Historical Society at Concord, cover eighteen large sheets written on both sides. The interest which attaches to it is, therefore, of no common sort, and may justify the copying of a couple of pages of the notes, as a good illustration of a method of work from which to his dying day he never departed.

Introduction. Memories of An. Greece. But Mod. Gr. one subject.

No Quixotic Emination. An American question, on large scale.

What is the nation? A reciprocation of message. No speeches & answers now.

If adopted it leaves everything to the President's unrestrained discretion. . . .

If the message be proper, this is not improper. Message, 18 page.

Our Policy.

1. Pacific growth, not acquisition. Time, peace & the arts, are our agents of greatness. No scheme so magnificent, as what our condition promises.

2. It is a liberal policy, not propagandists, but our side is known.

Age extraordinary; our situation peculiar; the best period & the best spot; our progress rapid, we must tax ourselves to keep up with it.

The great question is between absolute Govts.—and Regulated Govts.

Whether Soc. shall have a part in its own Govt. It is not content with kind masters.

The spirit of the age sets strongly in favor of free Govts.

This system is opposed in system by the Great Continent'l Powers. It is opposed wherever it shows itself, Naples, Piedmont, Spain and Greece. It is opposed for reasons rendering opposition to it as proper in this Country, as in Europe. It is opposed on settled principles.

The question is, *what opinions does it become this Country to express.*

But let us examine the truth of this. *Representation.* There is the Holy Alliance.

P. D. 32. 355 page   Holy Alliance, an extraordinary
       Sep. 1815.   & unnecessary League—Pufferdorf
—read abstract. Originated with Alex'n.—Shown in or'g'l drft. to L'd. Castlereagh, before it was shown to the other sovereigns. (L'd. C's. Speech, in P. D.)

But allowing a favorable construction to this, the Alliance has proceeded to Practical Resolutions, of dangerous import.

1. *All Constitutional rights proceed from the grants of Kings*—Intimated at the Federation—Charter.

The speech in behalf of the Greeks delivered and his resolution "laid in the tomb," Webster took but little active interest in public affairs, and turned his attention to private matters and to the duties that fell to his committees. Creditors under the Spanish treaty of 1819 had long been clamoring for their money, and a number of them had retained Webster to push their claims. The passage of a bill to discharge these debts was with him, as he says, "the great business of the session."

Such concerns as formed the daily business of the House did not interest him in the least, and he quickly fell into the habit of being present in body, but absent in mind. In a speech on the compensation bill of 1816 he had denounced this practice in strong terms. "There is," he said, "something radically defective in our system of government. No legislature in the world, however various its concerns or extensive its sphere, sits as long as this, notwithstanding that its sphere is so greatly contracted by the intervention of eighteen distinct legislatures. The system does not compel, on the part of its members, that attention which the nature of the public business requires. I refer to letters and papers on the desks of the members every day. They ought to have none of them. When a man comes into this House, he ought to leave on the threshold every feeling and thought not connected with the public service. Private letters and private conversation ought not to be permitted to encroach on the unity of his object. If in any way the attention of the House could be fixed on the speaker, there would be an end to long speeches, for I defy any man to address any assembly of this sort, and address them long, if their attention is fixed on him."

But Webster was older now; evil communications had corrupted his good manners, and he had become as great an offender as the worst, and, shutting his ears to the pleas and arguments of many a debater, would spend the hours writing letters. To the splendid opportunity which lay before one endowed with the qualities which make men leaders of their kind, he seems to have been blind. Never since the days of the War for Independence was a statesman of the constructive type more needed. The old parties founded and led by Washington and Jefferson were gone, and new ones to take their places were yet to be created. Of the issues then before the people all were sectional; none was national. That they would some day be united and become the basis of parties yet to be organized, and that the men who brought about this union of local interests would, for years to come, direct the policy and "sway the destiny of the country," was inevitable.

For work of this kind Webster was in no sense fitted. The abilities with which nature had so richly endowed him, his tastes, his studies, and his training pointed to no such career; and in the long run he was thrust aside and outrun by men of far less capacity, by demagogues who served the times, and, dying, left behind them no lasting work as the fruit of a long life spent in the public service. In the struggle for leadership which made memorable the next four years he was a mere looker-on, commenting now and then on the would-be Presidents and their chances of success. At New York, when on his way to attend Congress, he was amazed at the "sudden and extraordinary popularity of Mr. Clinton." New Jersey, he was inclined to think, would support Mr. Calhoun. At Washington every one was asking, "Will a caucus be held?" For twenty years past the Republican members of the House and Senate used to meet some February evening in each Presidential year and "recommend" to their fellow-citizens, as they said, two men to be President and Vice-President of the United States. The "recommendation" was often followed by the statement that the men named were recommended and in no sense nominated; that the recommendation was made in the interest of party unity and harmony and to prevent the wasteful scattering of electoral votes among a host of local favorites, not one of whom had the smallest chance of election. So long as the party was really united and the candidates chosen were men whose services in Revolutionary days entitled them to the grateful consideration of their countrymen, all went well. But now the party was not united: it was broken into many pieces, and as each fragment had rallied about a man of its own selection, a demand arose that the old method of nomination by the caucus should give way to the new one of nomination by the people.

Of this Webster heartily approved. "It appears to me to be our true policy," he wrote to Mason, "to oppose all caucuses, so far as our course seems to be clear. Beyond this I do not think we are bound to proceed at present. To defeat caucus nominations, or prevent them, and to give the election, wherever it can be done, to the people, are the best means of restoring the body politic to its natural and wholesome state." "One thing I hold to be material," he tells his brother: "get on without a caucus. It will only require a little more pains. It is time to put an end to caucuses. They make great men little and little men great; the true source of power is the people. The Democrats are not democratic enough; they are real aristocrats; their leaders wish to govern by a combination among themselves, and they think they have a fee simple in the people's suffrages. Go to the people and convince them that their pretended friends are a knot of self-interested jobbers, who make a trade of patriotism and live on popular credulity."

When at last the caucus is held and Crawford and Calhoun are nominated, he believes it "has hurt nobody but its friends. Mr. Adams's chance seems to increase, and he and General Jackson are likely to be the real competitors at last. General Jackson's manners are more Presidential than those of any of the candidates. He is grave, mild, and reserved. My wife is for him decidedly." A month later he is still convinced that

Jackson is "making head yet, Arbuthnot and Ambrister notwithstanding. The truth is, he is the people's candidate in a great part of the Southern and Western country. I hope all New England will support Mr. Calhoun for the Vice-Presidency. If so, he will probably be chosen, and that will be a great thing. He is a true man, and will do good to the country in that situation."

By the time the caucus was held, the House had settled down to the business of the session, and none that came before it was more important than the tariff. The act of 1816 had not produced the many benefits so hopefully expected. "This measure," said the high-tariff advocates, "was believed at the time to be all that was needed; but the immense accumulation in European markets of goods made by labor-saving machines operated by men and women content to live on potatoes, rice, and water, the exclusion of these goods from British markets and of British wares from European markets, forced the manufacturers of the Old World to seek our ports, where they have been only too well received. Their products, cheaply made and evading our tariff by fraudulent means, have been sold at the auction-block at prices which distance competition, and have been paid for with depreciated bank paper, which the foreign owners have exchanged for specie and carried from our country. This means the ruin of our banks, our manufactures, our farmers, and a decline in the value of land; for now that hundreds of thousands who consume food, liquor, fuel, and clothing, but produce them not, are out of employment, where will our farmers find a sale for the produce that they once sold readily at home?''

The hard times of 1819, the presence in the cities of great numbers of idle workmen, the activity of the Friends of National Industry, gave uncommon force to such arguments, and it soon became impossible for a dozen men to gather for any purpose without issuing an appeal for a new tariff. Grand juries presented the sale of British goods as a grievance. Political conventions called on voters to defeat such candidates for Congress as would not promise to work for a tariff. Public meetings discussed the need of protection, and as the day drew near when Congress must meet, petitions went about in every manufacturing town and village, and delegates from nine States assembled at New York. Calling themselves a convention of Friends of National Industry, they urged the formation of State societies to agitate for a tariff and to send representatives to a national convention to be held at New York city in 1820.

Nor were the enemies of a high tariff for protection less active. They, too, held meetings, and it was at one of these, gathered in Faneuil Hall, in 1820, that Webster spoke in behalf of a free-trade policy. Both sides were now in serious earnest, and during four years the issue was constantly before

Congress. The bill of 1820 was defeated by the casting-vote of the Vice-President; that of 1821 was not put upon its passage; the House refused to consider that of 1822: but when a fourth attempt was made in 1823, the Committee on Manufactures laid before the House a bill which the supporters of Webster expected him to resist. Personally he cared little for it; for the questions which filled his thoughts, occupied his hours of study, and which, to the last, he delighted to expound, were such as sprang from the interpretation of our Constitution, our principles of government, and not such as were concerned with political economy.

"On this same tariff we are now occupied," he writes; "it is a tedious, disagreeable subject. The House, or a majority of it, are apparently insane; at least I think so. Whether anything can be done to moderate the disease, I know not. I have very little hope. I am aware that something is expected of me; much more than I shall perform. It would be easy to make a speech, but I am anxious to do something better, if I can; but I see not what I can do." "The tariff is yet undecided. It will not pass, I think, in its present shape, and I doubt if it will pass at all. As yet I have not interfered much in the debate, partly because there were others more desirous to discuss the details than I am, and partly because I have been so much in the court. I have done, however, with the court, and the whole tariff subject is yet open. I shall be looking after it, though I should prefer it should die a natural death, by postponement or other easy violence.''

No such death awaited the bill, and when, one day in April, 1824, Clay took the floor and delivered that famous speech in which he outlined and defended his ''American policy,'' Webster knew that the time had come to reply. Never had Clay spoken more earnestly, more eloquently, or at greater length. He began at eleven in the morning and was still on his feet when the House adjourned at half-past three in the afternoon.

If tradition may be trusted, Webster went home that night fully determined to answer Clay, rose before daylight the next morning, and spent the time till the House met in jotting down on paper what he intended to say. But Clay, resuming the argument where he left it off the day before, spoke for several hours, and was then followed by a member from Mississippi, so that the afternoon was well spent when Webster began his reply, and was in turn forced to continue it on the following day. Tradition further tells us that, while he was then in the full swing of eloquence, a note was thrust into his hand, informing him that the great case of Gibbons against Ogden would be called for argument the next morning in the Supreme Court; that he ended his speech as speedily as possible, and went home, and to bed, and to sleep;

that he rose at ten that night, and, with no other
refreshment than a bowl of tea, toiled steadily till
nine the next morning, when his brief was done;
that he then partook of a slight breakfast of tea
and crackers, read the morning newspapers, went
to court, and there made that argument which destroyed the exclusive right to navigate the waters
of New York by steam, so long enjoyed by Fulton
and Livingston, and "released every creek and
river, every lake and harbor, in our country from
the interference of monopolies."

Many reasons combine to make the tariff debate of 1824 of no common interest. Neither
speaker, it is true, settled the controversy. More
than three quarters of a century has passed since
that day, yet the respective merits of free trade
and protection are as far as ever from settlement,
and still furnish plentiful material for campaigns
of education. Nevertheless, it must be admitted
that the principle and policy of protective tariffs
have never been better stated than in the brilliant
speech by Clay, nor more forcibly combated than
they were in the vigorous reasoning of Webster.
Clay made the better speech; Webster the better
argument. In the effort of Clay are plainly visible
all the characteristics of the man, both great and
small: his fervid patriotism, his glowing diction,
his lively imagination, his skill in grouping facts,
his superficial knowledge, and his inability to reason calmly to a logical conclusion. In the answer

7

of Webster are set forth the keen analysis, the deliberate reasoning, the full knowledge, the mastery of principles, which made him great. Nowhere else in our annals can be found two speeches of deeper interest to the student of economics.

Of the speech thus hastily prepared and hastily delivered, Webster had but a poor opinion. "We have heard a great deal of nonsense upon the subject," he wrote Mr. Mason, "and some of it from high quarters. I think you will be surprised at Mr. Clay's speech. My speech will be printed, and you will get it. Whatever I have done in other cases, I must say that in this I have published it against my own judgment. I was not expecting to speak at that time, nor ready to do so. And from Mr. Clay's ending I had but one night to prepare. The ideas are right enough, I hope, but as a speech it is clumsy, wanting in method, and tedious." His friends thought otherwise, and the mails soon began to bring him letters full of adulation and of praise for the Greek and tariff speeches. "I received a letter from a friend in London," says one correspondent, "dated the 6th of March, who justly observes: 'Mr. Webster's speech has been received with general approbation and applause. It has been translated into Greek and printed in London, in order to be distributed all over Greece. I am happy that the Demosthenes of America has taken the lead in encouraging and animating the countrymen of his great prototype.'

I tender my thanks for your lucid and magnificent speech on the Tariff. The ground you have assumed is the only one which history, policy, and experience can enable us to maintain with interest to the nation. I march with you side by side, in all the route you take. If you are not correct, there is no truth in *induction;* there is no *wisdom* among the learned; there is no *intelligence* to be found in Parliament; there is no reliance to be placed on the statements of the learned political writers on the economy of nations; in fact, we have not any *new lights* to guide us since the dark ages, and must grope on.''

CHAPTER VI

A NEW ENGLAND FEDERALIST

THE tariff disposed of, the only question of interest that remained was the coming election of a President. The long list of great names put before the voters in the course of three years by State legislatures, by conventions, by public meetings, by caucuses, by the members of Congress, had been cut down by time to four—Adams, Jackson, Crawford, and Clay. Could Webster have had his wish, Calhoun would have been the successor of Monroe. The great gulf that parted them in later years had not as yet begun to yawn. Again and again in his letters he calls the illustrious Carolinian "a true man." But the "will of the people" assigned to Calhoun the post of Vice-President, and of the four who remained as candidates for the Presidency the names of only three could come before the House of Representatives. That Adams, Jackson, and Crawford would be the three, Webster seems never to have doubted. Not once does he mention the name of Clay. Now he is sure that "the novelty of Gen'l Jackson is wearing off, and the contest seems to be coming back to the old question between Mr.

122

Adams and Mr. Crawford.'' ''The events of the
winter, with the common operation of time, have
very much mixed up Federalists with some other
of the parties, and though it is true that some men
make great efforts to keep up old distinctions, they
find it difficult. Mr. Adams, I think, sees also that
exclusion will be a very doubtful policy, and in
truth I think a little better of the kindness of his
feelings toward us than I have done. I have not
seen how Federalists could possibly join with those
who support Mr. C. The company he keeps at the
North is my strongest objection to him.''

There were those, however, who were not so
sure of ''the kindness of his feelings'' toward Federalists. That Mr. Adams would forget who it
was that condemned his conduct in the Senate,
chose a successor before his term had expired, and
forced him to resign seemed scarcely human.
That he would proscribe all Federalists was generally believed, and when, a little later, the failure
of the colleges to elect threw the choice of a President into the House, a member of the Maryland
delegation wrote to Webster for advice. The issue
thus presented to him was critical. In the election
by the House each of the four-and-twenty States
was to cast one ballot, and that ballot was to be
determined by the majority vote of the members
of the delegation. Maryland sent eight representatives, and so evenly were they divided by party
lines that the writer of the letter declared he be-

lieved that on his vote hung that of Maryland. The reply assured him that Adams would not proscribe old Federalists as a class, and to secure this assurance Webster called on the Secretary of State one evening and read the answer he proposed to send. In it were the words:

"For myself, I am satisfied, and shall give him my vote cheerfully and steadily. And I am ready to say that I should not do so if I did not believe that he would administer the government on liberal principles, not excluding Federalists, as such, from his regard and confidence. . . .

"I wish to see nothing like a portioning, parceling out, or distributing offices of trust among men called. by different denominations. . . . What I think just and reasonable to be expected is that, by some one clear and distinct case, it may be' shown that the distinction above alluded to does not operate as cause of exclusion." To this Adams objected. "The letter seemed to require him, or expect him, to place one Federalist in the administration. Here I interrupted him, and told him he had misinterpreted the writer's meaning. That the letter did not speak of those appointments called Cabinet appointments particularly, but of appointments generally. With that understanding, he said the letter contained his opinions."

Thus assured, the hesitating member from Maryland cast his vote for Adams, and so made Mary-

land one of the thirteen States that elected him.
Had Maryland supported Jackson, he would have
tied Adams, and the way would have been prepared for a prolonged contest. Something of this
sort was feared by Webster.

"As the 9th of February approaches," he wrote,
"we begin to hear a little more about the election.
I think some important indications will be made
soon. A main inquiry is, in what direction Mr.
Clay and his friends will move. There would
seem at present to be some reason to think they
will take a part finally for Mr. Adams. This will
not necessarily be decisive, but it will be very important. After all, I cannot predict results. I believe Mr. Adams might be chosen if he or his
friends would act somewhat differently. But if he
has good counselors, I know not who they are. I
would like to know your opinion of what is proper
to be done in two or three contingencies: 1. If on
the first of any subsequent ballot Mr. Adams falls
behind Mr. Crawford and remains so a day or two,
shall we hold out to the end of the chapter, or shall
we vote for one of the highest? 2. If for one of
the highest, say Jackson or Crawford, for which?
3. Is it advisable under any circumstances to hold
out and leave the choice to Mr. Calhoun? 4. Would
or would not New England prefer conferring the
power on Calhoun to a choice of General Jackson?"

The support of Clay was indeed important, and

the followers of Jackson, Adams, and Crawford were seeking it earnestly. Clay seemed, he himself says, "to be the favorite of every one"; "strong professions of high consideration and of unbounded admiration" met him at every turn; he was "transformed from a candidate before the people to an elector for the people." Deeply aware of the solemn duty thrust upon him, time was taken to weigh the facts on which a decision must be founded. While he deliberated, rumors of every sort were put afloat to awe and influence him; and when these failed, anonymous letters full of menace and abuse poured in on him daily. At last, when it could no longer be disguised that he would support Adams and not Jackson, a member of the House from Pennsylvania, in an unsigned note to a Philadelphia newspaper, declared that an "unholy coalition" had been formed; that Clay was to use his influence for Adams; and that Adams, if elected, was to make Clay Secretary of State. Lest Clay should not see the charge, a marked copy of the newspaper was sent him. He was stung to the quick, and, in a fit of rage, denounced the unknown writer in a Washington newspaper as "a base and infamous calumniator, a dastard, and a liar," and bade him disclose his name that he might be held responsible "to all the laws which govern men of honor." In plain words, he must meet the Speaker on the dueling-grounds at Bladensburg. Thus challenged, the

JOHN QUINCY ADAMS.

ANDREW JACKSON.

writer disclosed his name, and in a letter to the same Washington newspaper informed "H. Clay" that he would prove to the satisfaction of unprejudiced minds that a bargain had been made, and signed the note "George Kremer"—a representative from Pennsylvania.

What followed on the day that this card appeared has been described for us in lively terms by one who was present in the House.

The storm of war has at length burst forth. The card of Mr. Clay and the other card of Mr. Kremer have thrown all here into strong commotion. The morning on which the letter appeared everybody was talking about pistols and powder. Will he fight? Has he ever fought? Will he not excuse himself as coming from Pennsylvania? Where will they fight? These were the questions which everywhere struck the ear. When Mr. Clay entered the House every eye followed him. As to Kremer, he was in his seat two hours before the time of meeting. They gave no special sign of recognition, and soon after the morning business had proceeded, Mr. Clay rose and made the statement which you have since seen in the papers. Every tongue was hushed, and the house was still as an empty church. He spoke low and under evident stress of feeling. Mr. Kremer's assent to the proposed investigation was given in his usual high and sharp key (he is sometimes jocularly called Geo. Screamer), and then came the tug of war. The report gives a fair representation of what was said, but the manner, the tones, the gestures, the soul of the debate, no pen can convey. Kremer is a strong, broad-shouldered, coarse-looking Pennsylvania farmer, with a florid face and short, stiff, sandy hair. His dress is often slovenly; but his mind is sturdy and vigorous, and when much excited he utters a deal of plain sound sense, directly to the point.

The substance of Clay's speech was a request for a committee to investigate the charges, and when the committee was ordered, Mr. Kremer rose in his place and assured the House that he would appear and make good all he had said. But when the committee met and bade him present his proof, he refused to come, and denied the right of the House to take action. Webster wrote to his brother further in comment on this affair, and on the ludicrousness of the great Mr. Clay, of the "Harry of the West," Speaker of the House during six Congresses, hurrying off in the dusk of a cold winter morning to exchange shots with the eccentric member from Pennsylvania: "We have a little excitement here, as you will see; but there is less than there seems. Mr. Clay's ill-judged card has produced an avowal, or sort of avowal, which makes the whole thing look ridiculous. Mr. Kremer is a man with whom one would think of having a shot about as soon as with your neighbor, Mr. Simeon Atkinson, whom he somewhat resembles. Mr. Adams, I believe, and have no doubt, will be chosen, probably the first day."

In this he was quite right: Adams was chosen on the first ballot, and Webster was chairman of the committee sent to inform the Secretary of

State of his election by the House. Writing to Mr. Mason a few days after the House had elected Mr. Adams, and when the air was full of rumors of cabinet appointments, Webster again asserts his belief that Adams will be liberal.

"I took care to state my own views and feelings to Mr. Adams, before the election, in such a manner as will enable me to satisfy my friends, I trust, that I did my duty. I was very distinct, and was as distinctly answered, and have the means of showing precisely what was said. My own hopes at present are strong that Mr. Adams will pursue an honorable, liberal, magnanimous policy. If he does not, I shall be disappointed as well as others, and he will be ruined. Opposition is likely to arise in an unexpected quarter, and unless the administration has friends, the opposition will overwhelm it." One of the men—the one New England man— to whom rumor assigned a cabinet place, was Webster; but the report was without foundation. "It is not necessary," he wrote to Mr. Mason, "in writing to you, to deny the rumor, or rumors, which the press has circulated of a place provided for *me*. There is not a particle of probability of any such offer." His friends, however, would gladly have seen him in some position of more dignity than a seat in the House; and when the new Congress met and the old supporters of Crawford declared themselves ready to aid in putting a Federalist in the Speaker's chair, Webster was urged to become a candidate. "It was not a bad thing," he wrote, "that the friends of Mr. Crawford generally supported a Federalist for the Chair. Some of my friends thought I might have obtained a few votes for the place, but I wholly declined the attempt. If practicable to place me there, it would not have been prudent."

The compliment was a great one. From the discordant factions which by this time had quite destroyed the old Republican party of Jefferson two new parties were now about to be formed, the one to oppose, the other to support, the administration. Most careful leadership was needed, and the tender to Webster of the nomination to the speakership was the recognition of him by the friends of Adams, Clay, and Crawford as a broadminded and independent member, whose leadership men of widely different views were willing to follow. But again his love of law triumphed over his love of politics. To sit, day after day, in the Speaker's chair meant the loss of much business in the Supreme Court, the profit of which he could ill afford to spare, and the performance of a class of duties in the highest manner distasteful to him. The refusal to accept the speakership left him free to do as he pleased, and he became at once an interested spectator of the course of events.

The election over and Adams inaugurated, Webster went home to make ready for an event that added new luster to his fame as an orator. Al-

most fifty years had passed since the memorable
day in June, 1775, when the British thrice went
up and thrice fled down the slopes of Bunker Hill.
More than once during the half-century an attempt
had been made to mark the spot where Warren
fell with a monument worthy of the man and of
his comrades. While the colonies were still nomi-
nally under the crown, the provisional government
of Massachusetts gave permission to the lodge of
Masons over which Warren had presided to re-
bury his remains, provided "the colony" might
erect the monument to his memory. After the battle of Princeton had added one more to the list of
martyrs, the Continental Congress ordered that
two fine monuments should be erected—one at Boston to the memory of Warren, and one at Fred-
ericksburg to commemorate the death of General
Mercer. Neither was ever built, nor was any
marker placed till nearly twenty years after the
battle, when the King Solomon Lodge of Charlestown, at its own cost, put up a wooden pillar eighteen feet high, surmounted by a gilt urn and standing on a pedestal ten feet high. Still later, the
General Court of Massachusetts thought for a
while of a grand monument of American marble;
but it was left for the Bunker Hill Monument
Association, a band of patriotic citizens, to begin
the work in earnest. By them money was raised,
a design secured, preparations made to lay the
corner-stone on the fiftieth anniversary of the

battle, and Webster chosen orator of the day. He was then president of the association, and doubted the fitness of delivering the address; but his scruples were overcome, and, with the approval of Mr. Mason and his brother, he undertook the task.

The memorable parts of the oration—the magnificent opening, the address to Lafayette, the share in the fight he should assign to Prescott, the fine speech to the survivors of the battle, beginning "Venerable men!"—gave him much concern and were prepared most carefully. On the day this latter was composed he had gone with his son Fletcher and his man John "Trout" to fish in the waters of Mashpee.

"It was, as he states in his Autobiography, while middle deep in this stream [the Mashpee River] that Mr. Webster composed a great portion of his First Bunker Hill Address. He had taken along with him that well-known angler John Denison, usually called John Trout, and myself. I followed him along the stream, fishing the holes and bends he left for me; but after a while I began to notice that he was not so attentive to his sport or so earnest as usual. . . . This, of course, caused me a good deal of wonder, and, after calling his attention once or twice to his hook hanging on a twig or caught in the long grass of the river, and finding that, after a moment's attention, he relapsed again into his indifference, I quietly walked up near him and watched. He seemed to be gazing at the overhanging trees, and presently, advancing one foot and extending his right hand, he commenced to speak: 'Venerable men!' " The incident was often alluded to by Webster, and years afterward, when preparing a Fourth-of-July speech, he wrote to his son: "This morning, after breakfast and before Church, that is between half-past seven and eleven o'clock, I struck out the whole frame and substance of my address for the Fourth of July. I propose to write it all out, which I can do in three hours, and to read it, and to give correct copies at once to the printers. So, if I find a trout stream in Virginia, I shall not have to be thinking out 'Venerable Men! Venerable Men!' "

The ceremonies of the day were opened by the most imposing procession Boston had yet beheld. The militia in their uniforms, the masons in their regalia, the long array of societies of every sort with badges and banners, the presence in the line of two hundred veterans of the Revolution, of whom forty had manned the rude earthworks on Breed's Hill; the presence of Lafayette, through whom, as Webster truly said, the electric spark of liberty had been conducted from the New World to the Old; the shouting multitude that lined the way—all combined to make a scene as yet un-equaled.

Winding its way from the Common across the bridge to Charlestown, the procession halted first on Breed's Hill, where the corner-stone was laid with masonic ceremonies, and then went on to the north side, where, in the presence of as great a multitude as had ever gathered before an orator, Webster delivered his First Bunker Hill Address. He stood on a platform at the foot of the hill. Before him, seated on the hillside as if in a great amphitheater, or standing on the summit in a dense mass, was his audience, gathered from all the country round about.

The description of the ends the monument should serve, the address to the survivors of the war, the apostrophe to Warren, the eulogy of Lafayette, were greatly admired at the time. But there was one sentence which was more than admired, which sank deep into the memories of the people, exactly expressed their feelings, fired their patriotism, was transmitted from mouth to mouth, was quoted and cited again and again, furnished toasts and mottos for countless occasions, and came in an hour of trial to have a meaning far more serious than was in the mind of Webster when he said: "Let our object be, our country, our whole country, and nothing but our country."

With praises of his oration ringing in his ears, Webster set off to visit Niagara, and when December came was again in his old place in the House of Representatives. The times were full of interest. At last the "Virginia dynasty" was overthrown, and for the first time in four-and-twenty years an Eastern man was in the palace, "where," Mrs.

Webster writes to a friend, "things are under much better regulation than formerly. There is a little of Northern comfort. Instead of shivering in that immense cold saloon, we were shown into a good warm parlor, with a nice little white damsel to take care of our coats. I said there were no changes in the appearance of things here; there have been several new houses, which ought not to be passed over, but the distances are so immense they are hardly perceptible. The furniture at the palace below-stairs is precisely as it was. I believe all the appropriations have been confined to the second story. There are many things below that want renewing. I wish I could send you an inventory of the furniture as it was when Mrs. Adams came into possession—it 's a curiosity." Nor was Webster less impressed by the change. "The drawing-room," says he, "is agreed by all to have received great improvement. When I went there it was absolutely warm, within a very few degrees, to a point of comfort. I even saw gentlemen walking in the great hall of entrance, with apparent impunity, without their greatcoats on!" "Mr. Clay appears to get on very well in the discharge of his duties. I believe the whole diplomatic corps entertain much respect for him, and what I have seen of his diplomatic correspondence shows great cleverness." "Mr. Adams' mission to Panama is opposed in the Senate, and will be in the House when the money is asked for. It is

8

not unlikely it may be the first measure which shall assemble the scattered materials of opposition.''

During the summer of 1825, Mr. Clay had been waited on by the ministers of Mexico, Colombia, and Guatemala, who, in the name of their countries, invited the United States to send commissioners to a congress of republics at Panama. After some inquiry as to the subjects to be discussed, Adams accepted, and in the annual message announced that ''ministers will be commissioned to attend,'' and soon laid before the Senate the names of the three gentlemen he wished to serve. When the members of that body heard the words ''will be commissioned,'' the anger of all those who hated Adams flamed high. He had violated the constitutional right of the Senate. Without consulting it as to the fitness of such a mission, without placing before it one of the reasons which prompted him to such an act, he had decided the question and given the Senate merely the duty of confirming his appointments. This was a high-handed affront not to be endured, and when the Committee on Foreign Relations reported a resolution that it was ''not expedient'' ''to send any minister to the congress of American nations assembled at Panama,'' the attack on the President opened in earnest. As a question in constitutional government it interested Webster deeply, and he made up his mind, if the question reached the House, to ''make a short speech, for certain reasons, provided I can get out of court, and provided better reflection should not change my purpose,'' and gave his reasons to Mr. Mason.

"It happened, luckily enough, that the House of Representatives were occupied on no very interesting subjects during my engagements elsewhere. You see Panama in so many shapes that you probably expect to receive no news in regard to it. The importance of the matter arises mainly from the dead-set made against it in the Senate. I am afraid my friend Calhoun organized and arranged the opposition. *He expected to defeat the measure.* That would have placed the President in his power more or less, and if the thing could be repeated on one or two other occasions, *completely so.* Mr. Adams then would have been obliged to make terms, or he could not get on with the Government, and those terms would have been the *dismissal of Mr. Clay.* As far as to this point all parties and parts of the opposition adhere and cohere. Beyond this, probably, they could not move together harmoniously. Vast pains were taken, especially with new members, to bring them to a right way of thinking. Your neighbor was soon gained.

"At the present moment, some who acted a violent part in the Senate wish to have it understood that they are not, therefore, to be counted as members of a regular opposition. I have been informed that Mr. Woodbury and Mr. Holmes disclaim opposition. Others, again, say they had not full information, and complain of that. Others make quotations of sentences, words, or syllables from the documents and carp at them. But you see all. In H. R. [House of Representatives] it is likely the necessary money will be voted by 30 or 40 majority—we may have a week's debate.

"The real truth is, Mr. Adams will be opposed by all the Atlantic States south of Maryland. *So would any other Northern man*. They will never acquiesce in the administration of any President on our side the Potomac. This may be relied on, and we ought to be aware of it. The perpetual claim which is kept up on the subject of negro slavery has its objects. It is to keep the South all united and all jealous of the North. The Northwestern States and Kentucky are at present very well disposed; so is Louisiana. Tennessee and Alabama will agree to anything, or oppose anything, as General Jackson's interest may require. The Crawford men in Georgia will doubtless go in the same direction. In North Carolina there are some who prefer Mr. Adams to General Jackson, and in Virginia it may be doubted whether the general can be effectually supported. Virginia says little about the men whom she would trust, but opposes those actually in power. In our house, however, the Virginia phalanx of opposition is not formidable; more than a third, in number, may be reckoned favorable. There is some reason to think the Jackson fever begins to abate in Pennsylvania, and doubtless it is over in New Jersey. Under these circumstances, if New York and New England go steady, it is not likely that the South will immediately regain the ascendancy.''

A month later the long-promised speech was delivered, the action of the President defended, and the place of the executive in our system of government carefully explained. For the moment it seemed as if Webster was henceforth to be considered a supporter of the administration, and the mouthpiece of the President in the House. But such he was not to be. The duties of a representative had never been attractive. Quite as much of his time when in Washington had been given to cases in the Supreme Court as to the work in the House. He was famous as an orator and great as a lawyer, but men whose names have been long since forgotten surpassed him as congressmen. When, therefore, Mr. Rufus King resigned the British mission early in 1826, Webster eagerly sought the post, and in his usual way turned to Mr. Mason for advice.

''It seems to me,'' was the answer, ''that you cannot, under existing circumstances, assert your claim at the present time. Should the government offer you the appointment, I think you ought not to refuse it. But, if I mistake not, it will be thought you cannot at this time be spared from the House of Representatives. And as far as I understand the state of that body, I am inclined to think your presence there at the ensuing session very important.''

But the advice need never have been asked; the ink and the postage were wasted: for Adams never for one moment thought seriously of appointing Webster to any office, and he went home at the close of the session to be renominated and reëlected as the representative of the Boston district in the Twentieth Congress.

When Webster came again to Washington his reputation as an orator had been further increased by his ''Discourse in Commemoration of the Lives and Services of John Adams and Thomas Jefferson.'' The parts these two men had played in the founding of the republic had indeed been great and signal. Both had been members of the Continental Congress, and of the committee appointed to frame the Declaration of Independence. The one had written that famous document, the other had been its foremost defender, and both had signed it. Both had represented our country at foreign courts, each had been a leader of a great political party, and each had been raised first to the Vice-Presidency and then to the Presidency of the United States. Their deaths at any time would have been events of much public concern; but their deaths on the same day, and that day the fiftieth anniversary of the adoption of the Declaration of Independence, deeply impressed their countrymen as one of the remarkable coincidences in history. Commemoration services were held in many places, and for that at Boston the city council chose August 2, the fiftieth anniversary of the day on which the engrossed copy of the Declaration was laid upon the table of Congress to be signed, and invited Webster to deliver the oration.

A speech by such a man on such an occasion should have been delivered in the largest hall the city contained, or, in the open, from a platform on the Common. But the city fathers selected Faneuil Hall, draped it in black, packed the stage and floor with seats and settees, and when the procession had entered and the last seat was occupied shut the doors in the faces of the crowd without. Sure that there must be room within the hall, the people on the street first began to murmur, and then to shout and call, till Webster, coming to the edge of the platform, said, in a voice heard above the din: "Let those doors be opened!" He was obeyed, a rush followed, every inch of standing-room was quickly taken, and quiet restored.

The oration was much admired, and two passages in particular—the description of eloquence, and the imaginary debate between Adams and the opponent of independence—were thought unrivaled. Joseph Hopkinson assured Webster that the argument against the Declaration seemed to him much stronger than that in support of it. "This," said he, "confirms an opinion I have long held, that as things then stood, and putting the result out of the case, the strength of all human reasoning was with those who opposed the measure, although every elevated and noble feeling was in favor of it." "There were parts," Richard Rush wrote, on receiving his pamphlet copy of the oration, "that thrilled me. I read them to my family, and they thrilled them too. The speech beginning on page 38 made my hair rise. It wears the character of a startling historical discovery, that burst upon us at this extraordinary moment, after sleeping half a century. Curiosity, admiration, the very blood, all are set on fire by it. Nothing in Livy ever moved me so much. Certainly your attempt to pass the doors of that most august sanctuary, the Congress of '76, and become a listener and reporter of its immortal debates, was extremely bold, extremely hazardous. Nothing but success could have justified it, and you have succeeded." In time the speech, put into the mouth of Adams, found its way into school readers and speakers; was declaimed by three generations of young orators; was thought by many to have really been delivered in Congress, and twenty years after the day Webster moved his audience by the delivery of it in Faneuil Hall, letters still came to him asking if it was not genuine. Later still, when a member of Fillmore's cabinet, Webster was asked by the President what authority he had for putting the speech into the mouth of John Adams, when it was well known that the Continental Congress always sat behind closed doors. Webster answered that, save the character of the man and a letter to Mrs. Adams, he had none, and added, "I will tell you what is not generally known: I wrote that speech one morning, before breakfast, in my library, and when it was finished my paper was wet with my tears."

CHAPTER VII

THE ENCOUNTER WITH HAYNE

THE return of winter brought Webster back to Washington to enter on what proved to be his last months of service in the House of Representatives. On March 4, 1827, the term of Senator Mills of Massachusetts would end, and the health of that gentleman being far from good, it was certain that he would not be returned to the Senate. Against this Webster protested; but when the General Court met, the State Senate chose Levi Lincoln and sent his name to the House. Before that body could act, Mr. Lincoln positively refused to serve; so the election went over to the June session of 1827, when Webster was chosen by a large majority, and took his seat the following December. But he came to the capital a broken and disheartened man; for Mrs. Webster, who had accompanied him as far as New York, was unable to go farther, and died there in January, 1828. A long period of despondency followed. For months he could do nothing. To one friend he writes in his misery: ''I find myself again in the court where I have been so many winters, and surrounded by such men and things as I have usually found here. But I feel very little zeal or spirit in regard to passing affairs. My most strong propensity is to sit down and sit still; and if I could have my wish, I think the writing of a letter would be the greatest effort I should put forth for the residue of the winter." To another friend he declares: "I do not expect to find myself involved in a great pressure of affairs, and certainly shall do nothing that I am not absolutely obliged to do."

Out of this depressed and morbid state Webster was now lifted by the appearance in the Senate of the bill which laid the duties ever since known as the "tariff of abominations." The law of 1824, designed to protect the growers of wool and the makers of cloth, had failed signally, and had scarcely been two years upon the statute-book when the men in whose interests the tariff was laid were clamoring for its repeal. The wool-growers of Berkshire, the manufacturers of New England, the State of Massachusetts, whose delegation did not cast one vote for the tariff act of 1824, now sent long memorials to Congress. A committee representing the factory-owners appeared in Washington to lobby for the bill, and in January, 1827, such a bill as they wanted passed the House and was laid on the table of the Senate by the casting-vote of Calhoun. Both senators from Massachusetts, now become a tariff State, voted for the bill.

The closeness of the struggle was ominous, and each side, aroused and thoroughly in earnest, made ready for a renewal of the contest when Congress should meet again. Excited by the speeches of Robert Y. Hayne, James Hamilton, and Dr. Thomas Cooper, the people of South Carolina began "to calculate the value of our union," to ask "Is it worth our while to continue this union of States, where the North demands to be our master?" and filled their memorials with language of no uncertain kind, which North Carolina, Georgia, and Alabama more than reëchoed.

In the North a convention of Friends of Domestic Manufactures was held at Harrisburg, Pennsylvania, and a new tariff, based on its labors, was laid before the House of Representatives in 1828 —a tariff so hateful in its rates that its opponents were confident it would not pass. Indeed, it was carefully prepared to invite defeat, for a Presidential election was close at hand, and the friends of Jackson did not dare to go before the country as its executioners. In the first place, all duties were made high in order to please the protectionists of the Middle States and to keep them in the Jackson party. In the second place, whatever raw material New England used was heavily taxed. In the third place, it was agreed that Jackson men from both North and South should unite, prevent amendment, and force a vote on the bill with all its obnoxious duties. But when the yeas and nays were called on the passage of the bill, the Jackson men from the Southern States were to turn about and vote nay, and as it was believed that the men from New England would be forced to do likewise, the bill would be lost. As the Jackson men from the Northern States were to answer yea, the odium of defeat would rest on the supporters of Adams, and the followers of the Hero of New Orleans would appear as the advocates of the American system.

Unhappily, the plan failed; the House passed the bill, and threw the responsibility of rejection on the Senate.

In the debate which now followed, Webster did not intend to take part. He had just taken his seat as a new member; only a few weeks before he had come from the grave of his wife, and, crushed and heartbroken, felt "very little zeal or spirit in regard to passing affairs." But, as the discussion went on, and he heard senator after senator assail New England, and charge her with measures she had steadily resisted till resistance was vain; as he heard a senator from North Carolina speak of that State as "chained to the car of Eastern manufacturers," and describe "this new system" as "peculiar to aristocrats and monarchists"; as he heard Benton of Missouri assert that, as New England had originated all the tariff bills, she ought not now to complain of the burden they had laid on her commerce; as he heard Hayne of South Carolina declare that "in this business the interests of the South have been sacrificed, shamefully sacrificed, her feelings disregarded, her wishes slighted, her honest pride insulted''; as he heard him proclaim that "this system has created discordant feelings, strife, jealousy, and heart-burnings, which never ought to exist between the different sections of the same country.'' Webster saw that the hour had come to depart from his intention to be silent. Rising in his place, he said: "I have not had the slightest wish to discuss this measure, not believing that, in the present state of things, any good could be done by me in that way; but the frequent declarations that this was altogether a New England measure, a bill for securing a monopoly to the capitalists of the North, and other expressions of a similar nature, have induced me to say a few words.''

Such being his reasons, he denied that New England had ever been a leader in protection. He declared that from the adoption of the Constitution till 1824 she had held back and had held others back, because she believed that it was best that manufactures should make haste slowly; because she felt reluctant to build great interests on the foundation of government patronage; and because she could not tell how long that patronage would last, or with what sturdiness, skill, or perseverance it would continue to be granted. But the tariff of 1824 had settled the policy of the government, and nothing was left to New England but to conform herself to the will of others; nothing but to

consider that the government had fixed and determined its policy, and that its policy was protection. A vast increase of investments in manufactures had followed, and New England had fitted
her pursuits and her industry to the new condition.
Neither the principle on which the bill was founded,
nor the provisions which it contained, received his
approval; but the welfare of New England as a
whole was to be considered, and in the end he voted
for its passage. Just as the question was about to
be put, Hayne made a solemn protest against the
bill as a partial, unjust, and unconstitutional measure, and Webster answered him; but what he said
was not reported.

As the news of the passage of the bill and the
approval of the President spread over the country,
it was received with mingled feelings of approbation and disgust. In Massachusetts the vote of
Webster for the tariff was bitterly denounced and
as warmly defended. He seemed to have lost
ground, so his friends determined to give him a
great public dinner and afford him a chance to
explain his change of position. Faneuil Hall was
accordingly secured, and on the 5th of June, 1828,
he received his first public ovation. "On no
former occasion of festivity," says the Boston
"Chronicle," "has the old Cradle of Liberty been
so beautifully and splendidly decorated as it is to-
day in honor of the *Guest* whom the people of this
city delight to honor. The pillars are tastefully

embellished with evergreens, and the display of national flags is rich and variegated. From the center of the roof are suspended a number of flags of various colors, which come down in festoons, the ends hidden under the green foliage which winds the posts. The end fronting the door is ornamented (in addition to the two pictures of Washington and Faneuil) with a bust of John Adams, encircled with a wreath of flowers, under an arch, on the pillars of which are the names of our principal military and naval heroes. The arch is surrounded with the inscription, 'Our country, our whole country, and nothing but our country.' Over the doors are placed a ship, a plow, and a shearing-machine, indicating commerce, agriculture, and manufactures. On all sides of the Hall are banners belonging to the various societies and military companies of the city.''

The toasts, in the good old fashion of the time, were thirteen in number, and when the second was reached, and the toast-master read, ''Our distinguished guest—worthy the noblest homage which freemen can give, or a freeman receive, the homage of their hearts,'' the five hundred gentlemen gathered round the tables rose and gave forth shouts of welcome that were heard in the streets. The response of Webster was an explanation of his vote for the tariff and for the bill in aid of the soldiers of the Revolution. It was a defense of his position on internal improvements at federal expense,

JEREMIAH MASON.

EDWARD EVERETT.

JOSEPH STORY.

a condemnation of the political methods of the Jackson party, and a scornful reply to all who hated New England. The burden of the speech was, "Be not narrow-minded." "I was not at liberty," said he, "to look exclusively to the interests of the district in which I live, and which I have heretofore had the high honor of representing. I was to extend my views from Barnstable to Berkshire, to comprehend in it a proper regard for all interests, and a proper respect for all opinions." "It is my opinion, Mr. President, that the present government cannot be maintained but by administering it on principles as wide and broad as the country over which it extends. I mean, of course, no extension of the powers which it confers; but I speak of the spirit with which those powers should be exercised. If there be any doubt whether so many republics, covering so great a portion of the globe, can be long held together under this Constitution, there is no doubt, in my judgment, of the impossibility of so holding them together by any narrow, contracted, local, or selfish system of legislation. To render the Constitution perpetual (which God grant it may be), it is necessary that its benefits should be practically felt by all parts of the country and all interests in the country. The East and the West, the North and the South, must all see their own welfare protected and advanced by it."

While Webster in the summer of 1828 was warning his friends that the Union could not be preserved by a "narrow, contracted, local, or selfish system of legislation," the people of South Carolina, declaring the tariff to be just such a system, were hurrying on toward nullification and the disruption that Webster feared. When news of the passage of the bill reached that State, the flags on the shipping in Charleston harbor were put at half-mast; a great anti-tariff meeting was held, and addresses were made to the people of the State. The governor was urged to assemble the legislature at once; the press, with one voice, called on the people not to wear or use a "tariffed article," and not to buy a horse, a mule, a hog, or a flitch of bacon, a drop of whisky, or a piece of bagging from Kentucky; the Fourth-of-July toasts and speeches abounded in sentiments of sedition; and when the legislature met in the winter it adopted the "South Carolina Exposition of 1828," in which the doctrine of nullification was well and clearly stated by John C. Calhoun, and sent to Congress a memorial against the tariff. Beyond this the State legislature was not then ready to go; but the Exposition, in pamphlet form, was scattered over the South in the spring of 1829, and found its way in considerable numbers to the North. At last the State-Rights party had a platform drawn by the hand of a master and setting forth its principles boldly in unmistakable terms; and had its champions in Congress, and its supporters in every State below the Potomac and the Ohio rivers.

But where were the champions and the leaders
of the national party? Who was to frame a platform, state principles, and expound the Constitution for those whose motto was, "Our country,
our whole country, and nothing but our country"? That Webster had seriously meditated the
assumption of this task must not be doubted.
For thirty years the theme of all his speeches
had been love of country, devotion to the Union,
the grandeur and meaning of the Constitution.
He had preached it to the people of Hanover
while a college lad, to the people of Fryeburg while
a teacher in their school, to the "Federal Gentlemen of Concord" while a struggling lawyer yet
unknown to fame, and had embodied it in the Portsmouth oration in 1812. He had expounded the
Constitution in his Brentwood address, in his first
set speech in Congress, in the Dartmouth College
case, in the case of Gibbons against Ogden, and in
the oration on Bunker Hill; and in the eulogy on
Adams and Jefferson in glowing terms he had besought his countrymen to guard, preserve, and cher-
ish evermore the "glorious liberty," the "benign
institutions," of "our own dear native land."
That he should now behold unmoved the growing
sentiment of disunion in the South, that he should
read with indifference the "Exposition of 1828,"
is most unlikely. That he resolved to combat the
doctrine of nullification when the next occasion
offered, and that he prepared himself carefully, is

far more in accordance with his habits and his record. Certain it is that when the time came for an answer to the Exposition he was not unprepared to make it.

The first Congress during the administration of Jackson assembled on December 7, 1829, and for three weeks the Senate did little more than receive petitions and dispose of motions of inquiry. Not one of these motions provoked debate till, on December 29, Senator Foot of Connecticut offered his resolution, which reads: "Resolved, That the Committee on Public Lands be instructed to inquire into the expediency of limiting, for a period, the sales of public lands to such lands only as have heretofore been offered for sale and are subject to entry at the minimum price. And also, whether the office of Surveyor-General may not be abolished without detriment to the public interest." Scarcely had the clerk finished reading when Benton of Missouri was on his feet to demand the object which the mover had in view, and brought on a debate which ended in postponing consideration for a few days. When the resolution was at length taken up, a general discussion followed, and on the 18th of January, 1830, Benton delivered a great speech. During the debate a few days before he had taken occasion to denounce the resolution as an attempt to check immigration to the West; to declare it another outbreak of that hatred of the East for the West manifested over and over again in the course of the last four-and-forty years; and had declared that it was time "to face about and fight a decisive battle in behalf of the West." His speech was intended to open the conflict, and the charges of Eastern hostility were now fully stated. To shut the emigrant out of the West and attempt to keep the magnificent valley of the Mississippi a haunt for wild beasts and savage men, instead of making it the home of liberty and civilization, was an injury to the people of the Northeast and to the oppressed of all states and nations. To force poor people in the Northeast to work as journeymen in the manufactories, instead of letting them go to new countries, acquire land, and become independent freeholders, was a horrid and cruel policy. The manufacturers wanted poor people to do their work for small wages. These poor people wished to go West, get land, have their own flocks and herds, orchards and gardens, meadows and dairies, cribs and barns. How to hinder it, how to prevent their straying off in this manner, was the present question. The late Secretary of the Treasury could find no better way than by protection to domestic manufactures—a most complex scheme of injustice, which taxed the South in order to injure the West and pauperize the poor of the North. That was bad enough, but it was lame, weak, and impotent compared with the scheme now on the table of the Senate—a scheme which proposed to stop the further survey of land, limit the sales to the refuse of innumerable pickings, and break the magnet which was drawing the people of the Northeast to the blooming regions of the West. Mr. Benton then went on to specify six "great and signal attempts to prevent the settlement of the West," and ended by saying that the hope of the West lay not in itself, but "in that solid phalanx of the South and those scattering reinforcements in the Northeast" which, in times past, "had saved the infant West from being strangled in its birth."

The debate had now become exciting, and in the course of the next day Mr. Hayne of South Carolina took part. He reviewed the land policy of England, France, and Spain in colonial times, praised its liberality, denounced the meanness of the United States, and drew a dismal picture of the way our government stripped the settler on the public lands of all his money, and then spent it, not in the betterment of the West, but in the East, and so entailed on the hardy frontiersman, for years to come, universal poverty, lack of money, paper banks, relief laws, and all the evils, social, political, and moral, such a system was sure to produce.

"But, sir," he exclaimed, "there is another purpose to which it has been supposed the public lands can be applied, still more objectionable. I mean that suggested in a report from the Treasury Department under the late administration, of so regulating the disposition of the public lands as to create and preserve in certain quarters of the Union

a population suitable for conducting great manufacturing establishments. . . . Sir, it is bad
enough that government should presume to regulate the industry of man; it is sufficiently monstrous
that they should attempt, by arbitrary legislation,
artificially to adjust and balance the various pursuits of society, and to organize the whole labor
and capital of the country. But what shall we say
of the resort to such means for these purposes?
What! create a manufactory of paupers, in order
to enable the rich proprietors of woolen- and cot-
ton-factories to amass wealth? From the bottom of
my soul do I abhor and detest the idea that the
powers of the federal government should ever be
prostituted for such purposes."

While Benton was making his attack on the East,
Webster was not present in the Senate, and as no
newspaper published speeches the day after they
were made, Webster neither heard nor knew what
Benton said. But he did hear Hayne, and took
notes of the speech, and on the following day made
what is known as his first reply to Hayne. Nothing, said he, was further from "my intention than
to take any part in the discussion of this resolution, . . . yet opinions were expressed yesterday on the general subject of the public lands, and
on some other subjects, by the gentleman from
South Carolina, so widely different from my own
that I am not willing to let the occasion pass without some reply. In the first place, the gentleman

from South Carolina has spoken of the whole course and policy of the government toward those who have purchased and settled the public lands as wrong. He held it to have been from the first harsh and rigorous. He was of the opinion that the United States had acted toward those who subdued the Western wilderness in the spirit of a stepmother; that the public domain had been improperly regarded as a source of revenue; that we had rigidly compelled payment for that which ought to have been given away.

"Now, sir, I deny altogether that there has been anything harsh or severe in the policy of the government toward the new States in the West. The government has been no stepmother to the new States. She has not been careless of their interests, nor deaf to their requests; but from the first moments when the Territories which now form these States were ceded to the Union down to the time in which I am now speaking, it has been the invariable object of the government to dispose of the soil according to the spirit of the obligations under which it was acquired, to hasten its settlement, and to rear the new communities into equal and independent States. From the very origin of the government these Western lands and the just protection of the settlers have been the leading object of our policy. The Indian titles have been extinguished at the expense of many millions. Is that nothing? These colonists, if we are to call them so, in passing the Alleghany did not pass beyond the care and protection of their own government. Wherever they went, the public arm was still stretched over them. Are the sufferings and misfortunes under Harmer and St. Clair not worthy to be remembered? Do the occurrences connected with military efforts show an unfeeling neglect of Western interests?''

Webster next passed in review the four sources of the public lands—the cessions by the States to the old Congress, the compact with Georgia in 1802, the purchase of Louisiana in 1803, and the purchase of Florida in 1819; stated at length the conditions of the cessions by the States; proved that, bound by these conditions, Congress could not give away the lands; and passed to another observation of Hayne's which ''did not a little surprise'' him.

The gentleman from South Carolina was anxious to get rid of the lands because the permanent revenue derived from them tended to corrupt the people and to consolidate the government. ''Consolidation,'' said Webster in reply—''that perpetual cry both of terror and delusion—consolidation! When gentlemen speak of the effects of a common fund belonging to all the States as having a tendency to consolidate the government, what do they mean? Do they mean, or can they mean, anything more than that the union of the States will be strengthened by whatever furnishes inducements to the people of the States to hold together? This is the sense in which the framers of the Constitution use the word consolidation. This, sir, is General Washington's consolidation. This is the true constitutional consolidation. I wish to see no new powers drawn to the general government; but I confess I rejoice in whatever tends to strengthen the bond that unites us and encourages the hope that our Union may be perpetual. I know that there are some persons in the part of the country from which the honorable member comes who habitually speak of the Union in terms of indifference, or even of disparagement. They significantly declare that it is time to calculate the value of the Union.[1] The Union to be preserved while it suits local and temporary purposes to preserve it, and to be sundered whenever it shall be found to thwart such purposes. Union of itself is considered by the disciples of this school as hardly a good. It is only regarded as a possible means of good, or, on the other hand, as a possible means of evil. I deem far otherwise of the Union of the States, and so did the framers of the Constitution. What they said, I believe—fully and sincerely believe—that the Union of the States is essential for the prosperity

[1] At a meeting at Columbia in the summer of 1827, Thomas Cooper, president of the South Carolina College, said in a speech: "I have said that we shall, ere long, be compelled to calculate the value of our Union, and to inquire of what use to us is this most unequal alliance by which the South has always been the loser and the North always the gainer. Is it worth while to continue this Union of States when the North demands to be our masters and we are required to be their tributaries?"

and safety of the States. I am a Unionist. I would strengthen the ties that hold us together. Far indeed in my wishes, very far distant, be the day when our associated and fraternal stripes shall be severed asunder, and when that happy constellation under which we have risen to so much renown shall be broken up and be seen sinking, star after star, into obscurity and night!''

Webster now came ''to that part of the gentleman's speech which has been the main occasion of my addressing the Senate. The East! the obnoxious, the rebuked, the always reproached East! We have come in, sir, on this debate, for even more than a common share of accusation and attack. If the honorable member from South Carolina was not our original accuser, he has yet recited the indictment against us with the air and tone of a public prosecutor. He has summoned us to plead on our arraignment, and he tells us we are charged with the crime of a narrow and selfish policy, of endeavoring to restrain emigration to the West, and, having that object in view, of maintaining a steady opposition to Western measures and Western interests. And the cause of this selfish policy the gentleman finds in the tariff. . . . Sir, I rise to defend the East. I rise to repel both the charge itself and the cause assigned for it. I deny that the East has at any time shown an illiberal policy toward the West. I pronounce the whole accusation to be without the least foundation.

. . . I deny it in general, and I deny each and all its particulars. I deny the sum total, and I deny the details. I deny that the East has ever manifested hostility to the West, and I deny that she has adopted any policy that would naturally lead her in such a course. But the tariff! the tariff! Sir, I beg to say, in regard to the East, that the original policy of the tariff is not hers, whether it be wise or unwise. New England is not its author. It was literally forced upon her, and this shows how groundless, how void of all probability, any charge must be which imputes to her hostility to the growth of the Western States as naturally flowing from a cherished policy of her own.''

Having delivered this point-blank and vigorous denial, Webster went on to cite the many benefits the East had conferred on the West—the excellent land system, the ordinance of 1787 which made free soil of the Northwest Territory, the Cumberland Road, the Portland Canal—and closed by moving an indefinite postponement of Mr. Foot's resolution.

But scarcely was he seated when Benton rose and began a reply. He was still speaking when the Senate adjourned for the day.

As the news of Webster's speech spread through the city, great excitement was manifest. That Webster, whose coolness and political sagacity were proverbial, should deliberately pass over Benton, and, singling out Hayne, should answer him, as-

tounded the members from the West and the South.
Among the Southern and Western members of both
houses, says the New York "Evening Post," the
sensation produced was so great that on the next
day, when Hayne was expected to reply, there was
scarce a quorum in the House of Representatives.
The Senate gallery was packed, the lobbies were
choked, and ladies, invading the floor of the Senate, took the seats of the senators, till the clerk's
desk and the Vice-President's chair, it was jokingly
said, were the only spots they did not occupy.

In the presence of this eager and expectant multitude a member rose and asked that the resolution
be postponed till Monday next, as Webster, who
wished to be present at the discussion, had engagements out of the Senate and could not conveniently
remain. Hayne objected. "I see the gentleman
from Massachusetts in his seat, and presume he
could make an arrangement which would enable
him to be present. I will not deny that some things
have fallen from the gentleman which rankled here
[touching his breast], from which I would desire
at once to relieve myself. The gentleman has discharged his fire in the face of the Senate. I hope
he will now afford me the opportunity of returning
the shot." While Hayne paused for a reply, Webster rose from his seat and, folding his arms, said,
with all the dignity he could command: "I am
ready to receive it. Let the discussion proceed."
Benton then continued his speech of the day before,

while Webster left the Senate to obtain the postponement of his business in court. An hour later he returned, whereupon Benton, who was still speaking, stopped, and yielded the floor to Hayne, who at once began his famous reply. The day was then far spent, and as candle-light was drawing near, Hayne, after an hour's speech, gave way for a motion to adjourn till Monday, the 25th of January. We are told by those who were in Washington at the time that as the report that Hayne was answering Webster passed from mouth to mouth, strangers, citizens, and members of Congress could scarcely wait in patience for the three days which must pass before the Senate would again assemble; and that, when the Monday so eagerly wished for came, the mass of humanity struggling for admission to the Senate Chamber surpassed anything ever seen before. "Nothing," says one witness, writing on the evening of the memorable day, "could exceed the crowd which assembled to-day in the Senate to hear the expected speech of Mr. Webster in reply to Mr. Hayne; but Mr. Hayne, keeping all the vantage in his power, occupied the ground until the hour of adjournment, and all that could be heard or seen of Mr. Webster was at the last moment, when he rose and claimed and obtained the floor for to-morrow. Mr. Hayne spoke fluently, warmly, energetically. He, of course, convinced all who were politically opposed to Mr. Webster (or who, out of envy of the luster of his fame, would willingly see his brightness dimmed) that he had obtained a triumph; and such as heard him through, and as may leave the city to-morrow morning before Mr. Webster can obtain the floor to reply, will doubtless go away with the full conviction that such is the fact. To-day there was no possibility of squeezing into the Senate Chamber after the commencement of the discussion, and to-morrow, I presume, it will be quite as difficult, for I have never witnessed a more intense curiosity than that which now prevails to watch every movement in this political rencounter.''

Hayne began by saying that when he threw out his ideas as to the policy of the government in regard to the public lands he little thought that he should be called on to meet such an argument as had been made by the senator from Massachusetts. The gentleman from Missouri, it was true, had charged the Eastern States with an early and continued hostility toward the West. But the member from Massachusetts, instead of making up the issue with the gentleman from Missouri, had chosen him as an adversary, and poured out the vials of wrath on his devoted head. Not content with this, the Massachusetts senator had gone on to assail the South and call in question the principles and conduct of South Carolina. Why was this? Had the gentleman discovered in former controversies with the senator from Missouri that he was over-matched? Did he hope for an easy victory over a more feeble adversary? Was it his object to thrust the member from South Carolina between the gentleman from Missouri and himself, in order to rescue the East from the contest it had provoked with the West? If so, he should not be gratified.

Passing from what Webster did to what Webster said, Hayne charged him with inconsistency, taxed him with holding one view as to the public land policy in 1825, and a very different one in 1830; denied that New England had always been friendly to the West; asserted that prior to 1825 she had opposed appropriations for internal improvements in the West, and declared that the change in feeling was a result of the coalition of 1825. Then it was, said he, that the "happy union between the members of that celebrated coalition was consummated, whose immediate issue was the election of a President from one quarter of the Union, with the succession, as it seemed, secured to another. The American System, before a rude, disjointed, and misshapen mass, now assumed form and consistency; then it was that it became the settled policy of the government that this system should be so administered as to create a reciprocity of interests and a reciprocal distribution of government favors: East and West, the tariff and internal improvements, while the South—yes, sir, the impracticable South—was to be out of your protection."

As one of the fruits of the liberal and paternal policy of the government toward the West, Webster had cited the history of Ohio; had drawn a picture of her in 1794, when a fresh, untouched, unbounded, and magnificent wilderness; and another of her in 1830, an independent State, with one million of inhabitants; and had pointed with pride to the fact that in the march of progress she had left behind her a majority of the old States, had taken her place beside Virginia and Pennsylvania, and in point of numbers would soon admit no equal but New York. Later in his speech, Webster touched on the beneficent effects of free soil on the growth of States and the increase of population north of the Ohio, and asked, Had an antislavery ordinance been applied to Kentucky before Boone crossed the gap of the Alleghany, would it not have contributed to the ultimate growth of that commonwealth?

Combining these two, Hayne charged him with contrasting the weakness of slave-holding States with the superior strength of free States, retorted with a defense of slavery, made a comparison of the happy lot of slaves on the plantations and the poor, wretched, vile, and loathsome lot of free negroes in Northern cities, denied that the South was weak, denied that it feared slave uprisings, asserted that slave labor had enriched the whole country and the North far more than the South, claimed that slavery had never yet been injurious to individual or national character, and in evidence cited the long roll of sons of the South from Washington to Jackson.

10

Passing to Webster's remarks on consolidation, Hayne reviewed the history of the Federalists and the National Republicans, declared they were one and the same, and denounced them as men who looked on the Constitution as forming not a federal but a national union and regarded consolidation as no evil. He next fell upon Webster's record on the tariff, and then charged him with having crossed the border, with having invaded the State of South Carolina, with making war on her citizens, and with having sought to overthrow her principles and her institutions. He then reviewed the history of South Carolina and the history of Massachusetts from the days of the Revolution to those of the Hartford Convention, and, having done this, asked who were the friends of the Union? Those who would confine the federal government strictly within the limits prescribed by the Constitution, who would preserve to the States and the people all powers not expressly delegated, who would make this a federal, not a national, union; or those who favored consolidation, who were constantly stealing power from the States to add strength to the federal government, and who undertook to regulate the whole industry and capital of the country?

Hayne now plunged into a defense of the South Carolina doctrine of nullification. It was, he said, the good old republican doctrine of '98; the doctrine of the Virginia resolutions of '98; of the Kentucky resolutions of '98 and '99, and of Madison's report of '99; it was the pivot of the political revolution of 1800; the doctrine of Thomas Jefferson; of the Boston memorial of 1809, and of Webster when he wrote his pamphlet on the embargo and delivered a celebrated speech against that measure in the House of Representatives. The doctrine that the federal government is the exclusive judge of the extent, as well as the limitations of its powers seemed to him utterly subversive of the sovereignty and independence of the States. It made very little difference whether Congress or the Supreme Court were vested with this power. If the federal government, in any or all of its departments, could fix the limit of its own authority, and the States be bound to submit to its decision, then were the States reduced to mere corporations and the government made one without limitation of powers.

When Hayne finished, the clock in the chamber was marking the hour of four, and Webster having obtained the floor for the following day, the Senate adjourned.

Next morning the Senate room was, if possible, more crowded than ever, and the murmur which swept over it when Webster stood up having died away into silence, he turned toward Calhoun, who occupied the chair, and said: "Mr. President, when the mariner has been tossed for many days in thick weather, and on an unknown sea, he naturally avails himself of the first pause in the storm, the earliest glance of the sun, to take his latitude and ascertain how far the elements have driven him from his true course. Let us imitate this prudence, and, before we float farther on the waves of this debate, refer to the point from which we departed, that we may at least be able to conjecture where we are. I ask for the reading of the resolution before the Senate.''

The resolution having been read by the secretary, Webster observed that it was almost the only subject about which something had not been said by the gentleman from South Carolina in his speech running through two days. Every topic in the wide range of public affairs, past or present, general or local, seemed to have attracted Mr. Hayne's attention, save only the resolution under debate. To the public lands he had not paid even the cold respect of a passing glance. Webster then restated his position as to the use of public lands, and refuted the charge of inconsistency; upheld the policy of the government in disposing of its lands; defended its right to engage in internal improvements, and answered Hayne's questions when, how, and why New England supported measures favorable to the West. He charged Hayne with stretching a drag-net over the whole surface of political pamphlets, indiscreet sermons, frothy paragraphs, and fuming popular addresses; over whatever the pulpit in its moments of alarm, the press in its heats, and parties in their extrava-

ROBERT Y. HAYNE.

gance had thrown off in times of general excitement. He declined then, or at any time, to separate this farrago into its parts and answer and examine its components, and came at last to the "grave and important duty" of stating and defending what he understood "to be the true principles of the Constitution under which we are here assembled."

"I understand the honorable gentleman from South Carolina to maintain," said Webster, "that it is a right of the State legislature to interfere whenever, in their judgment, this government transcends its constitutional limits, and to arrest the operation of its laws.

"I understand him to maintain this right as a right existing under the Constitution; not as a right to overthrow it, on the ground of extreme necessity, such as would justify violent revolution.

"I understand him to maintain an authority on the part of the States thus to interfere for the purpose of correcting the exercise of power by the general government, of checking it, and of compelling it to conform to their opinion of the extent of its powers.

"I understand him to maintain that the ultimate power of judging of the constitutional extent of its own authority is not lodged exclusively in the general government, or any branch of it; but that, on the contrary, the States may lawfully decide for themselves, and each State for itself, whether, in a given case, the act of the general government transcends its power.

"I understand him to insist that if the exigency of the case, in the opinion of any State government, require it, such State government may, by its own sovereign authority, annul an act of the general government which it deems plainly and palpably unconstitutional."

This, he said, was the sum of what he understood to be the South Carolina doctrine. "I call this the South Carolina doctrine only because the gentleman himself has so denominated it. I do not feel at liberty to say that South Carolina, as a State, has ever advanced these sentiments. I hope she has not, and never may." But "that there are individuals besides the honorable gentleman who do maintain these opinions is quite certain. I recollect the recent expression of a sentiment which circumstances attending its utterance and publication justify us in supposing was not unpremeditated. 'The sovereignty of the State—never to be controlled, construed, or decided on but by her own feelings of honorable justice.'"

That the people have an inherent right to resist unconstitutional laws without overthrowing their government Webster said he did not deny. But who should decide on the constitutionality or unconstitutionality of laws? This depended on the origin of the government and the source of its power. "Is it," said he, "the creature of the State legislatures or the creature of the people? If the agent of the State governments, then they might control it, provided they could agree on the manner. If the United States government were the agent of the people, then the people, and the people alone, could control, restrain, modify, reform it. According to the gentleman from South Carolina, it was the creature not only of the States, but of each State severally, so that each might assert for itself the power to settle whether it acts within the limits of its authority. It was the servant of four-and-twenty masters, of as many different wills and purposes, yet bound to obey all. This absurdity arose from a misunderstanding of the source of the government. It is, sir," said Webster, "the people's government, made for the people, made by the people, and answerable to the people. . . . I hold it to be a popular government, erected by the people, those who administer it responsible to the people, and itself capable of being amended and modified just as the people may choose it should be. It is as popular, just as truly emanating from the people, as the State governments. It is created for one purpose, the State governments for another. It has its own powers; they have theirs. There is no more authority with them to arrest the operation of a law of Congress, than with Congress to arrest the operation of their law. The people erected this government. They gave it a Constitution, and in that Constitution they have enumerated the powers which they bestow on it. They have made it a limited government. They have defined its authority. But no definition can be so clear as to avoid possibility of doubt. No limitation can be so precise as to elude all uncertainty. Who, then, shall construe this grant of the people? Who interpret their will when it may be supposed to be left in doubt? For this the people have wisely provided in the Constitution itself, when they declared that the judicial power should extend to all cases arising under the Constitution and laws of the United States. The very end, the chief design for which the Constitution was framed and adopted was to set up a government that should not be forced to act through State agency or depend on State discretion. The people had enough of that kind of government under the Articles of Confederation. Are we in that condition still? Are we yet at the mercy of State discretion?

"Sir, I deny this power of State discretion altogether. Gentlemen may say that in an extreme case a State government might protect the people from intolerable oppression. Sir, in such a case the people might protect themselves without the aid of State governments. Such a case warrants revolution. Talk about it as we will, these doctrines go the length of revolution. They lead directly to disunion and civil commotion, and therefore it is that I enter my public protest against them.

"When my eyes shall be turned to behold for the last time the sun in heaven, may I not see him shining on the broken and dishonored fragments of a once glorious union; on States dissevered, discordant, belligerent; on a land rent with civil feuds, or drenched, it may be, in fraternal blood! Let their last feeble and lingering glance rather behold the gorgeous ensign of the republic, now known and honored throughout the earth, still full high advanced, its arms and trophies streaming in their original luster, not a stripe erased or polluted, nor a single star obscured, bearing for its motto no such miserable interrogatory as, 'What is all this worth?' nor those other words of delusion and folly, 'Liberty first and Union afterward,' but everywhere spread all over it in characters of living light, blazing on all its ample folds as they float over the sea and over the land, and in every wind under the whole heavens, that other sentiment dear to every true American heart—Liberty and Union, now and forever, one and inseparable.''

CHAPTER VIII

THE scenes about the Capitol as the debate went on can best be described by those who beheld them. Says one: "I never saw the Senate Chamber so completely taken possession of as it has been since Monday. Long before the hour of meeting, in defiance of a keener northwester than we have experienced since last winter, fairy forms were seen to glide through the cold avenues of the Capitol, as eager to obtain a seat favorable for hearing the expected effusions of master minds as if much more than a moment's gratification were at stake; and by the time the Chair had called to order, the Chamber was filled to overflow." Says another: "Mr. Webster's last speech on Mr. Foot's resolution was one of the most splendid oratorical efforts we have ever heard. Though General Hayne is asserted by the friends of the present administration to possess no ordinary talents, he appeared to a painful disadvantage in comparison with Mr. Webster, whose intellectual power was perhaps never so happily exhibited on any former occasion. At the close of his last speech there was an involuntary burst of admiration in the galleries. His eulogy on South Carolina, his panegyric of Dexter, and his peroration, were unrivaled. His sarcasm was biting; his illustrations happy and luminous; his reasoning conclusive and unanswerable. Never was an adversary so completely and entirely demolished. Every position which General Hayne had taken was prostrated, and his very weapons were thrown back upon him with a deadly force. The Senate seemed to hang upon the lips of the orator with intense pleasure, and the audience, numerous beyond all former example, paid a just tribute to his genius and power by the admiration which they expressed.'' A third assures us: ''Business in the House lags, the various speakers addressing themselves to almost empty benches since Mr. Webster obtained the floor. He concluded his speech to-day, and it is universally admitted to have been one of the greatest efforts of which the human mind is capable. That it will add to the reputation of Mr. Webster, high as it now stands, no one can doubt. This effort has placed him at an unapproachable distance from all competitors. Faction and prejudice may try to prop the fame of the Bentons, the Haynes, and others, at the expense of Mr. Webster; but there is not an intelligent individual who has listened to this sharp encounter who has not gone from the chamber of legislation fully convinced that Mr. Webster is by far the greatest man in Congress. You cannot walk the streets this afternoon, you cannot enter the door of a mess-room, you cannot approach the fire in the bar-room of a hotel, but you hear this language from every mouth, accompanied with expressions of regret that Mr. Hayne and Mr. Benton should have entered into such an unholy alliance, and have made this premature movement for the purpose of pulling down the East, and planting the South in its room, in the affections of the Western States. This speech of Mr. Webster has occupied about six hours in the delivery, and were it possible to transfer to paper the manner in which it was delivered, to infuse with every report the tone of sarcasm, the curl of the lip, the flush of the cheek, the flash of the eye, by which the language of the orator was frequently enlivened, elucidated, and enforced, then, but not till then, could those who have had no opportunity of hearing this speech be made sensible of the banquet which they have lost.''

"Opinions as to the victory in this strife are of course as much divided as are the parties, whose different views of the Constitution have been severally maintained, and by worthy champions. The opposition party generally contended that Mr. Webster overthrew Mr. Hayne, while, on the other hand, the result is triumphantly hailed by the friends of the administration as a decisive and complete victory over the Eastern Giant. They say the Southern orator is more than a match for the New England lawyer. Mr. Hayne is truly an ora-

tor full of vehemence, eloquence, and passion, a
correct and powerful reasoner, with a most vivid
imagination, graceful in person and action, and
with a most musical voice. Mr. Webster, on the
other hand, is a lawyer, and a great lawyer, one
who has at his immediate command all the logic
and all the wariness of a cool and practised debater, of extensive reading and much learning, of
perfect self-possession and always master of the
subject, and ready with coolness and circumspec-
tion to seize upon the weak points of his adversary. As a speaker, he is calm, collected, and dignified, sometimes energetic, but never impassioned
or vehement. His voice is clear and firm. His
gestures are few, and not always graceful. A material contrast between the two men is in the expression and mobility of their features. Mr. Webster's countenance is generally cold, severe, and
impassive, which makes the occasional sarcasm,
when accompanied by a sneer or a smile, exceedingly effective. The face of Mr. Hayne is constantly in motion; every varying emotion is distinctly visible.

"To those who, without being influenced by any
previous opinions of the comparative powers of
these gentlemen, shall compare this speech with
that to which it was an answer, its superiority in
point of oratorical ability will be manifest. The
management of the argument in relation to the public lands is exceedingly happy. The retort on the

subject of the tariff is tremendous. The answer to Mr. Webster's unprovoked attack on the South is managed with great skill.''

The great reply of Webster, in the opinion of this critic, was that of a skilful and able debater closely pressed by his opponent, but fighting hard. ''The opening is wanting in dignity. The retort on the subject of Mr. Hayne's allusion to Banquo's ghost is a good instance of the dexterous use of the weapons of logic. The Hartford Convention and the course of New England during the embargo and the war are not defended at all. The most unfortunate part of the speech is that where Mr. Webster attempts to excuse his course on the subject of the tariff. The most prudent course for Mr. Webster would have been not to break the silence on this subject which he had hitherto preserved.''

While comment of this sort was passing from newspaper to newspaper over the country, nobody save those who crowded the Senate Chamber knew what either Hayne or Webster said. A few journals of prominence, and with wide circulation for those days, maintained at the capital correspondents whose daily or weekly letters appeared as soon as the mail could carry them; and it was from such writers that the country first heard of the Webster-Hayne debate. But for the full reports of the speeches, the press the country over was dependent upon the Washington newspapers, and in this instance the reports were deliberately held back for revision. "We do not know," says the editor of the Philadelphia "Gazette" of February 15, "what has become of Mr. Hayne's and Mr. Webster's speeches." Not till the 17th of February was he able to print a small part of Hayne's reply of January 21, with the remark, "We have at length received from Washington the first part of Mr. Hayne's speech"; and not till February 25, just thirty days after it was delivered, did the people of Philadelphia read the opening passage of Webster's second reply to Hayne. In March it was printed in the New York "Evening Post," and the month was well advanced before it appeared in Boston.

But Webster's friends and admirers did not wait for the report of the second speech to flood him with praise. As the report of his first speech went abroad, each mail brought letters full of enthusiasm. "I must beg the favor of you," says a Baltimore admirer, "to forward me a copy or two of your speech by the first mail after it is committed to press. I congratulate you most cordially and sincerely upon your triumph in the most signal manner, not only in the estimation of your friends, but of your opponents, who are forced to acknowledge it. From the date of that speech I shall date the rise and successful progress of liberal and enlightened principles in our country. The reign of ignorance must be short and the march of intellect most certain."

"The glorious effect of your patriotic, able, and eloquent defense of New England," writes another, "and the triumphant support you have given to the fundamental principles of the Constitution, are not confined to the capital of the Union. The aroma comes to gladden our hearts, like the spicy gales of Arabia to the distant mariner.

"Never have I heard such universal and ardent expressions of joy and approbation. You have assumed an attitude which the adverse times demanded, and nobly braved the storm that threatened the destruction of our liberties. The dignity and independence of your manner, and the time, all were calculated to produce a result auspicious to our destinies."

"I am," says a third, writing from Columbia, South Carolina, "a son of New England, and proud to claim you as her champion. The friends of Mr. Hayne will be very active in circulating his second speech on Foot's resolution, and I am anxious to have the antidote to circulate with the bane. You would therefore oblige me by sending me your rejoinder. Receive my warm acknowledgments for your able and manly defense of *my country*, the country of Yankees."

"The demand for copies of Mr. Webster's speech," said the editor of the "National Intelligencer," at whose office it was printed in pamphlet form, "has been unprecedented. We are just completing an edition of twenty thousand copies, which, added to a former edition, will make an aggregate of very nearly forty thousand copies issued from this office alone. There have also been printed at other places in the United States perhaps twenty different editions of these speeches. It is hardly too much to say that no speech in the English language was ever so universally diffused or so generally read.''

Of the many orations which up to this time had been delivered in the Senate of the United States, the most far-reaching and enduring was the second reply to Hayne. At last the South Carolina doctrine had been fittingly answered; at last the Union had found a stanch defender, the Constitution a noble interpreter, and the friends of both a champion able to give utterance to the thoughts and feelings they could not so well express. His words sank into their hearts, his speech became a mine of political wisdom, and the Constitution henceforth had for them a new meaning.

Nor was the effect on Webster less important. He became at once a truly national character, saw the Presidency almost within his grasp, and from that day forth was animated by a ceaseless longing to become one of the temporary rulers of his country. National politics,—nay, even local political affairs,—the conduct of his possible competitors, his own course on the issues of the day, now had for him a weight and moment such as he had never accorded them before. His fellow-country-

11

men everywhere became eager to hear and see him. When Congress rose, a public dinner was tendered by his Boston admirers, and declined. A publisher, without his consent, announced a collection of his speeches. An admirer in Boston sent him a silver pitcher as a testimony of gratitude "for your services to the country, in your late efforts in the Senate, especially for your vindication of the character of Massachusetts and of New England."

When, a few months later, he went to New York City to try a case before the United States Circuit Court he was the lion of the hour. Men, and even women, who had never before been near a court came by scores, filled the room, and stood in crowds about the door to get a glimpse of him. Later yet, when the autumn election was about to be held in Massachusetts, and it was announced that Webster would address the electors in Faneuil Hall, men came from Salem, Worcester, and many parts of the State to hear him. So great was the crowd that the doors were forced in long before the hour of meeting. It was Saturday night, and after he had spoken for three hours the meeting was adjourned to Sunday evening, when he again addressed an immense gathering in Center Hall, over the New Market. In the course of this two-day speech, Webster, while condemning Jackson's veto of the Maysville Road Bill, said: "I know no road that the administration would call national. All roads are in some degree local. They run over a particular territory and connect particular districts. No road runs everywhere except, except—" Here, says the report, Mr. Webster had wound himself up in a sentence from which he was apparently unable to extricate himself—"except—" "The road to ruin," said Mr. Otis. "Except the road to ruin," said Webster, "and this is an administration road," and the hall rang with applause.

As Webster's countrymen began to realize more and more that South Carolina was really in earnest; that a great political issue had been raised that was not easily to be put down; that the Constitution and the Union were really at stake; and that his reply to Hayne was something more than a fine speech defending New England, their eagerness to hear him on this issue grew apace, and invitations to speak came to him from many quarters. That from New York was accepted, and in March, 1831, at a public dinner over which Chancellor Kent presided, Webster again argued against nullification, and again maintained that the final arbiter was the Supreme Court. "The general and State governments, both established by the people, are established for different purposes and with different powers. Between those powers questions may arise, and who shall decide them? Some provision for this end is absolutely necessary. Where shall it be? This was the question before the convention, and various schemes were suggested. It was foreseen that the State might inadvertently pass laws inconsistent with the Constitution of the United States or with acts of Congress. How should these laws be disposed of? Where shall the power of judging, in cases of alleged interference, be lodged? One suggestion in the convention was to make it an executive power, and to lodge it in the hands of the President, by requiring all State laws to be submitted to him, that he might negative such as he thought appeared repugnant to the general Constitution. . . . It was not pressed. It was thought wiser and safer, on the whole, to require State legislatures and State judges to take an oath to support the Constitution of the United States, and then leave the States at liberty to pass whatever laws they pleased; and if interference, in point of fact, should arise, to refer the question to judicial decision. To this end, the judicial power under the Constitution of the United States was made coextensive with the legislative power. It was extended to all cases arising under the Constitution and the laws of Congress. The judiciary became thus possessed of the authority of deciding, in the last resort, in all cases of alleged interference between the State laws and the Constitution and laws of Congress. . . .

"On the occasion which has given rise to this meeting, the proposition contended for in opposition to the doctrine just stated was that every State, under certain supposed exigencies and in certain supposed cases, might decide for itself and act for itself, and oppose its own force to the execution of the laws. By what argument, do you imagine, gentlemen, was such a proposition maintained? . . . As I understand it, when put forth in its revised and most authentic shape, it is this: that the Constitution provides that any amendments may be made to it which shall be agreed to by three fourths of the States; there is, therefore, to be nothing in the Constitution to which three fourths of the States have not agreed. All this is true; but then comes this inference, namely, that when one State denies the constitutionality of any law of Congress, she may arrest its execution as to herself, and keep it arrested, till the States can be consulted by their conventions and three fourths of them shall have decided that the law is constitutional. Indeed, the inference is still stronger than this; for State conventions have no authority to construe the Constitution, though they have authority to amend it, therefore the argument must prove, if it prove anything, that when any one State denies that any particular power is included in the Constitution, it is to be considered as not included, and cannot be found there till three fourths of the States agree to insert it. . . .

"Seeing the true grounds of the Constitution thus attacked, I raised my voice in its favor, I must confess with no preparation or previous intention. I can hardly say that I embarked in the contest from a sense of duty. It was an instantaneous impulse of inclination, not acting against duty, I trust, but hardly waiting for its suggestion. . . . Gentlemen, I have true pleasure in saying that I trust the crisis has in some measure passed by. The doctrine of nullification has received a severe and stern rebuke from public opinion.''

The rebuke, unhappily, went unheeded; the crisis had in no sense passed away, for the spirit of nullification rose higher and higher with each succeeding month. State Rights and Free Trade associations were formed over all South Carolina; a great celebration was held by the State Rights and Free Trade party at Charleston on the Fourth of July, 1831; and a convention at Columbia just before Congress met in December, and a convention of delegates from the State Rights and Free Trade associations at Charleston on Washington's Birthday, 1832. The meaning of these demonstrations was not misunderstood. Congress made haste to offer concessions, and in July, 1832, passed an act altering and amending the tariff law of 1828—the ''tariff of abominations.'' But it was far from what South Carolina demanded; it was still a tariff for protection, and in October her legislature called a convention which, it was understood, would nullify the tariff laws. Meanwhile Calhoun once more came forward to explain the right and duty of the State to take such action. In the course of the previous summer he had written and published in a newspaper an "Address to the People of South Carolina," in which the doctrine of State Rights and the relation of the States to the federal government was reargued. Governor Hamilton had never read a word of the address, though it had been before the people for over a year; but now, when some excuse must be found for another paper by the Vice-President, the Governor found time to read it through, and wrote to urge its author to state his doctrine with more detail. Calhoun consented, and the letter was at once made public.

The moment Webster read it he determined to reply, and as the Vice-President had put his argument in the form of a letter to the Governor of South Carolina, a leading nullifier, Webster decided to put his argument in the form of a letter to Chancellor Kent, a great expounder of the Constitution. "Mr. Calhoun, as you are doubtless aware," he wrote the chancellor, "has published a labored defense of nullification in the form of a letter to Governor Hamilton. It is far the ablest and most plausible, and therefore the most dangerous, vindication of that particular form of revolution which has yet appeared. In the silence of abler pens, and seeing, as I think I do, that the affairs of this government are rapidly approaching a crisis, I have felt it to be my duty to answer Mr. Calhoun; and as he adopted the form of a letter in which he put forth his opinions, I think of giving my answer a similar form. The object

of this is to ask your permission to address my
letter to you. I propose to feign that I have received a letter from you calling my attention to
Mr. Calhoun's publication, and then, in answer to
such supposed letter, to proceed to review his whole
argument at some length, not in the style of a
speech, but in that of cool, constitutional, and legal
discussion. If you feel no repugnance to be thus
written to, I will be obliged to you for your assent.''

The chancellor readily assented. ''I shall deem
it an honor,'' said he, ''to be addressed by you
while engaged in the investigation of such an interesting subject. . . . The crisis is indeed
portentous and frightful. We are threatened with
destruction all around us, and we seem to be fast
losing our original good sense and virtue. . . .
If we are to be saved, we shall be largely indebted
to you.'' To write the letter at once was not possible. ''I cannot,'' said Webster, ''complete the
paper before the election.''

But there was one other man whose opinion on
the question of nullification was much more important just then than was the opinion of Calhoun,
and that man was the President. Suppose South
Carolina were to carry out her threat and actually
nullify the tariff acts, would the President execute
those laws? Would he have the duties collected
at the port of Charleston? Webster was inclined
to think he might not. In a recent veto message
Jackson had said: ''Each public officer who takes

an oath to support the Constitution swears that he will support it as he understands it, and not as it is understood by others." Taking this for a text, Webster told the National Republicans assembled in convention at Worcester in October, 1832, that "the general adoption of the sentiments expressed in this sentence would dissolve our government. It would raise every man's private opinions into a standard for his own conduct. . . . Mr. President, how is it possible that a sentiment so wild and so dangerous, so encouraging to all who feel a desire to oppose the laws and to impair the Constitution, should have been uttered by the President of the United States at this eventful and critical moment? Are we not threatened with dissolution of the Union? Are we not told that the laws of the government shall be openly and directly resisted? Is not the country looking with the utmost anxiety to what may be the result of these threatened courses? . . . Mr. President, I have very little regard for the law or the logic of nullification. But there is not an individual in its ranks capable of putting two ideas together who, if you will grant him the principles of the veto message, cannot defend all that nullification has ever threatened.

"To make this assertion good, sir, let us see how the case stands. The legislature of South Carolina, it is said, will nullify the late revenue or tariff law because *they say* it is not warranted by the

Constitution of the United States *as they understand the Constitution*. They, as well as the President of the United States, have sworn to support
the Constitution. Both he and they have taken the
same oath in the same words. Now, sir, since he
claims the right to interpret the Constitution as he
pleases, how can he deny the same right to them?
. . . How can he answer them when they tell
him that the revenue laws are unconstitutional *as
they understand the Constitution*, and that, therefore, they will nullify them? . . . Sir, the
President of the United States is of opinion that an
individual called on to execute a law may himself
judge of its constitutional validity. Does nullification teach anything more revolutionary than that?
The President is of opinion that judicial interpre-
tations of the Constitution and the laws do not bind
the consciences and ought not to bind the conduct
of men. Is nullification at all more disorganizing
than that? The President is of opinion that every
officer is bound to support the Constitution only
according to what ought to be, in his private opinion, its construction. Has nullification, in its wild-
est flight, ever reached to an extravagance like that?
No, sir, never. . . . But let me ask, sir, what
evidence there is that the President is himself opposed to the doctrines of nullification—I do not
say to the political party which now pushes these
doctrines, but to the doctrines themselves. Has he
anywhere rebuked them? Has he anywhere dis-

couraged them? Has his influence been exerted to
inspire respect for the Constitution, and to produce
obedience to laws? . . . Alas, sir, we have seen
nothing, nothing of all this. . . . Now, sir,
I think it exceedingly probable that the President
may come to an open rupture with that portion of
his original party which now constitutes what is
called the Nullification party. I think it likely he
will oppose the proceedings of that party if they
shall adopt measures coming directly in conflict
with the laws of the United States. But how will
he oppose? . . . How will the President attempt to put down nullification, if he shall attempt
it at all? We are told, sir, that the President will
immediately employ the military force, and at once
blockade Charleston. . . . For one, sir, I raise
my voice beforehand against the unauthorized employment of military power, and against supersed-
ing the authority of the laws by an armed force,
under pretense of putting down nullification. The
President has no authority to blockade Charleston;
the President has no authority to employ military
force till he shall be duly required so to do by
law and by the civil authorities. His duty is to
cause the laws to be executed. His duty is to support the civil authority."

The one way to put down nullification, Webster
believed, was to defeat the reëlection of Jackson,
"and place the government in the hands of its
friends." But Jackson was not defeated, and on

him lay the burden of dealing with practical, not theoretical, nullification. The legislature of South Carolina called a State convention; the convention declared that the tariff acts of 1828 and 1832 were null and void, and fixed the 1st of February, 1833, as the day on and after which they should no longer be "binding on this State, its officers or citizens." The legislature then made all preparations necessary to put nullification into effect, and what had so often been threatened, so many times discussed, and so little really feared seemed certain to happen at the end of January.

CHAPTER IX

THE ENCOUNTER WITH CALHOUN

SOUTH Carolina having done her part, it was now for the federal government to make the next move, and the Executive, with characteristic energy, moved quickly. The annual message in December, 1832, contained but one short paragraph on affairs in South Carolina, and the tone of what was said was hailed by the nullifiers as conciliatory to them, and as a sure indication that the President had no thought of using force. Adams described it as going "to dissolve the Union into its original elements"; as "a complete surrender to the nullifiers of South Carolina." Clay called it "ultra on the side of State Rights." But ere a week went by the President followed up the message with a proclamation which astonished both friends and foes alike, and left neither his opinions nor his intentions any longer in doubt. "The Constitution of the United States," said Jackson to the followers of Hayne and Calhoun, "forms a government, not a league; and whether it be formed by compact between the States or in any other manner, its character is the same. . . . I consider the power to annul a law of the United

States incompatible with the existence of the
Union, contradicted expressly by the letter of the
Constitution, and destructive of the great object
for which it was formed. To say that any State
may at pleasure secede from the Union is to say
that the United States are not a nation." Language of this sort contained the very essence of
the reply to Hayne, and the moment Webster read
it he determined to uphold any vigorous measure
Jackson might propose. When the proclamation
reached Boston, a great meeting to denounce nullification was about to be held in Faneuil Hall,
and to the men so gathered Webster consented to
speak on the subject of the proclamation. "Having been detained at home a few days after the
meeting of Congress," said he, "by the necessity
of attending to some private affairs, I have been
induced to delay my departure for another day,
that I might be present at this meeting of my fellow-citizens. . . . I regard the issuing of this
proclamation by the President as a highly important occurrence. . . . Mr. Chairman, the
general principles of the proclamation are such as
I entirely approve. I esteem them to be the true
principles of the Constitution. It must now be
apparent to every man that this doctrine of nullification means resistance to the laws, by force.
It is but another name for civil war. The President has declared that in meeting the exigencies of
this crisis it is his determination to execute the

laws, to preserve the Union by all constitutional means, to arrest, if possible, by moderate but fair measures, the necessity of a recourse to force. . . . In all this I most cordially concur,'' and ''in this way of meeting the crisis I shall give the President my entire and cordial support. . . . Our only alternative is to preserve the Union one and entire, as it now is, or else to break up and return to the condition of separate States, with the unpromising chance of forming hereafter new, partial, sectional, rival, perhaps hostile governments, thus bidding adieu forever, not only to the glorious *idea,* but to the glorious reality of the United States of America.''

In South Carolina the proclamation was received with indignation and contempt by the people and the press, was answered, at the request of the legislature, by Hayne (now governor in place of Hamilton), by the election of Calhoun to the United States Senate in place of Hayne, and by the passage of such acts as were necessary to put nullification into effect. The proclamation had fallen on deaf ears, and no hope of a peaceable settlement remaining, Jackson, about the middle of January, 1833, asked for authority to collect the revenue in South Carolina by force if necessary— a request to which the Senate responded with the Revenue Collection Bill—the ''Force Act'' or ''Bloody Bill,'' as the nullifiers called it. In the opinions of the State Rights men, this bill was the worst that had ever been reported by a committee to the Senate. It struck down the States, made a dictator of the President, and repealed the Constitution, the true meaning of which Calhoun now explained in three resolutions. The people of the several States composing these United States, so read the first resolution, are united as parties to a constitutional compact, to which each State acceded as a separate sovereign community, and the union of which the compact is the bond is a union between the States that have ratified it.

The second declared that the people of the several States in thus creating a general government delegated to it certain definite powers, reserving, each State to itself, the residuary mass of powers; that whenever the general government assumes the exercise of powers not delegated by the compact, its acts are of no effect; and that, as in all other cases of compact without any common judge, each has the right to judge for itself as well of the infraction as of the mode and measure of redress.

The third aimed directly at the proclamation, declared that the people of the United States did not form a nation, that the States had not surrendered their sovereignty, that the citizens of the States had not transferred their allegiance to the general government, and that all assertions to the contrary were without foundation in truth and contrary to the most certain historical facts and the clearest deductions of reason.

The resolutions having been printed and then laid on the table, debate on the "Bloody Bill" was resumed. As the discussion went on day after day for two weeks, the fact became clear that even the steadfast friends of the President could not be relied on to support the measure. They opposed it bitterly,—nay, denounced it, as Webster said, "with the same vehemence as they used to do when they raised their patriotic voices against what they called a 'coalition.'" It smelled, they declared, like the Alien and Sedition laws, was as bad as the Boston Port Bill, brought back the horrors of the Jersey prison-ships, made the President sole judge of the Constitution, sacrificed everything to arbitrary power, and was worse than the Botany Bay Law of Great Britain. The party of Jackson, in short, was in revolt, and the President at this crisis turned to Webster for support. Members of Congress urged him to defend the bill, and when he seemed indifferent, one of the cabinet called at his lodgings and asked for his help. To this appeal he complied, and a few days later, in the Senate, took occasion to say that he would support the measure as an independent member "discharging the dictates of his own conscience." "I am," said he, "no man's leader; and, on the other hand, I follow no lead but that of public duty and the star of the Constitution. I believe the country is in considerable danger; I believe an unlawful combination threatens the integrity of the Union. . . .

12

I think the people of the United States demand of us, who are intrusted with the government, to maintain that government. . . . For one, I obey this public voice; I comply with this demand of the people. I support the administration in measures which I believe to be necessary; and while pursuing this course I look unhesitatingly, and with the utmost confidence, for the approbation of the country.''

This alliance of Webster with the Jackson party was of serious importance. It was now certain that in the struggle over the Force Bill he would bear a part; and, with the recollection of the debate with Hayne fresh in memory, the followers of Calhoun looked forward to the contest with uneasiness. No other man in the Senate, save Clay, then approached Webster in influence with the people; and to Clay Calhoun now turned for assistance, which the great Kentuckian proved only too willing to give. He would not speak for the bill; he would not vote for it; he would not do anything to strengthen the hands or add to the prestige of the man who believed in the coalition, who had proscribed the friends of ''Harry of the West,'' and had defeated him so overwhelmingly in the election just passed. But, worse than all, the father of the American System, the great apostle of protection, would yield to South Carolina, and had in his desk the draft of a bill designed to abandon the protective system, yield every point South Caro-

THOMAS H. BENTON.

JOHN C. CALHOUN.

HENRY CLAY.

lina demanded, and reduce the tariff to a revenue basis. This bill Clay introduced soon after his interview with Calhoun.

With Clay thus silenced and committed to the course of the nullifiers, but two of the great triumvirate remained to contend, the one for "our country, our whole country, and nothing but our country"; the other for nullification, secession, and disunion. Calhoun opened the contest, and Webster followed with the speech known in his collected works as "The Constitution not a Compact between the States."

We are told that as Webster was about to leave his lodgings to make that speech, the carriage of the President drew up at the door, that the private secretary of Jackson stepped out, delivered a message, and then drove the senator to the Capitol steps. But how changed the scene from those memorable days three years before! No citizens streamed with hasty steps from every street and avenue. No crowd blocked the entrance, filled every aisle and gallery and lined the walls of that little chamber associated with so much that is dramatic in our history. Calhoun was to continue his speech of the day before, a performance which had greatly disappointed his friends. Never at any time had he been considered an orator, and long absence from legislative halls had dulled what little power as a speaker he once possessed. More than fifteen years had rolled by since he accepted the place of Secretary of War under Monroe, and in all that time Calhoun had addressed no legislative body. He was, says one who now heard him, quite unfit for long and sustained effort by reason of the intensity of his feelings, a lack of physical power, and a weak voice. He was hoarse and indistinct in utterance. Calhoun finished a little before one o'clock, and a moment later Webster secured the floor, and spoke for two hours and a half, when the Senate took a recess till five o'clock. Meantime the news that Webster was answering Calhoun spread through the city, and when the Senate reassembled the chamber was "crowded to suffocation." The House had adjourned for the day, and the members were now to be seen seated among the senators. Citizens eager to hear a great speech had hurried to the room with wives and daughters, had filled every available inch of space, and furnished an audience far different from that of two hours before. From five till eight o'clock, when the speech ended, Webster spoke with much of his old power, carried his listeners with him, and when he closed, "a long, loud, and general clapping of hands rose from the floor and galleries." The cause was greater than any ever before put on trial. The preservation of the Union, the success of democratic government, the ability of a people spread over half a continent to rule themselves, was to be decided once and forever. Reject the Force Bill, and government by the many was supplanted by the rule of a few; the Constitution was degraded from an instrument of government to the contract of a league, and the Republic of the United States was no more worthy to be called a nation. Pass the Force Bill, and the supremacy of law was upheld firmly, nullification was brought down from a peaceful remedy to a revolutionary right, and the Union made stronger than ever. Webster began by saying: "I shall not, Mr. President, follow the gentleman step by step through the course of his speech. Much of what he has said he has deemed necessary to the just explanation of his own political character and conduct. On this I shall offer no comment. . . . But the gentleman's speech made a few days ago, when introducing his resolutions, those resolutions themselves, and parts of his speech just now concluded may probably be justly regarded as comprising the whole South Carolina doctrine. I shall not consent, sir, to make any new Constitution, or to establish another form of government. I will not undertake to say what a constitution for these United States ought to be. That question the people have decided for themselves, and I shall take the instrument as they have established it, and shall endeavor to maintain it, in its plain sense and meaning, against opinions and notions which, in my judgment, threaten its subversion.

"The first two resolutions of the honorable gentleman affirm these propositions, viz.:

"1. That the political compact under which we live, and under which Congress is now assembled, is a compact to which the people of the several States, as separate and sovereign communities, are the parties.

"2. That these sovereign parties have a right to judge, each for itself, of any alleged violation of the Constitution by Congress, and, in case of such violation, to choose, each for itself, its own mode and measure of redress.

"It is true, sir, that the honorable member calls this a 'constitutional' compact, but still he affirms it to be a compact between sovereign States. . . . Sir, I must say to the honorable gentleman that in our American political grammar 'constitution' is a noun substantive; it imparts a clear and distinct idea of itself; and it is not to lose its importance and dignity, it is not to be turned into a poor, ambiguous, senseless, unmeaning adjective for the purpose of accommodating any new set of political notions. Sir, we reject his new rules of syntax altogether. We will not give up our forms of political speech to the grammarians of the school of nullification. By the Constitution we mean not a 'constitutional compact,' but simply and directly the Constitution, the fundamental law; and if there be one word in the English language which the people of the United States understand, this is that word. . . . We know what the Constitution is, we know what the plainly written fundamental law is, we know what the bond of our union and the security of our liberty is, and we mean to maintain and defend it in its plain sense and unsophisticated meaning. . . .

"The first resolution declares that the people of the several States 'acceded' to the Constitution, or to the constitutional compact, as it is called. This word 'accede,' not found either in the Constitution itself or in the ratification of it by any one of the States, has been chosen for use here doubtless not without a well-considered purpose.

"The natural converse of accession is secession, and therefore when it is stated that the people of the States acceded to the Union, it may be more plausibly argued that they may secede from it. If, in adopting the Constitution, nothing was done but acceding to a compact, nothing would seem necessary, in order to break it up, but to secede from the same compact. But the term is wholly out of place. . . . The people of the United States have used no such form of expression in establishing the present government. They do not say they accede to a league, but they declare they ordain and establish a Constitution. Such are the very words of the instrument itself; and in all the States, without an exception, the language used by their conventions was that they 'ratified the Constitution.' . . . Sir, I intend to hold the gentleman to the written record. In the discussion of a constitutional question I intend to impose upon him the restraints of constitutional language. The people have ordained a Constitution; can they reject it without revolution? They have established a form of government; can they overthrow it without revolution? These are the true questions. . . .

"The gentleman's resolutions, then, affirm in effect that these twenty-four United States are held together only by a subsisting treaty, resting for its fulfilment and continuance on no inherent power of its own, but on the plighted faith of each State. . . . If, sir, this be our political condition, it is time the people of the United States understood it. Let us look for a moment to the practical consequences of these opinions. One State, holding an embargo law unconstitutional, may declare her opinion and withdraw from the Union. She secedes. Another, forming and expressing the same judgment on a law laying duties on imports, may withdraw also. She secedes. . . . But, sir, a third State is of opinion not only that these laws of impost are constitutional, but that it is the absolute duty of Congress to pass and maintain such laws, and that by omitting to pass and maintain them its constitutional obligations would be grossly disregarded, . . . and for this violation of the Constitution she may threaten to secede also. Virginia may secede and hold the fortresses in the Chesapeake. The Western States may secede, and take to their own use the public lands. Louisiana may secede if she chooses, form a foreign alliance, and hold the mouth of the Mississippi. If one State may secede, ten may do so—twenty may do so. Sir, as these secessions go on one after another, what is to constitute the United States? Whose will be the army? Whose the navy? Who will pay the debts? Who fulfil the public treaties? Who perform the constitutional guarantees? Who govern this District and the Territories? Who retain the public property? . . . This, sir, is practical nullification.

"And now, sir, against all these theories and opinions I maintain:

"1. That the Constitution of the United States is not a league, confederacy, or compact between the people of the several States in their sovereign capacities, but a government proper, founded on the adoption of the people and creating direct relations between itself and individuals.

"2. That no State authority has power to dissolve these relations, that nothing can dissolve them but revolution, and that consequently there can be no such thing as secession without revolution.

"3. That there is a supreme law, consisting of the Constitution of the United States, acts of Congress passed in pursuance of it, and treaties; and that in cases not capable of assuming the character of a suit in law or equity, Congress must judge of and finally interpret this supreme law so often as it has occasion to pass acts of legislation; and in cases capable of assuming, and actually assuming, the character of a suit, the Supreme Court of the United States is the final interpreter.

"4. That an attempt by a State to abrogate, annul, or nullify an act of Congress, or to arrest its operation within her limits, on the ground that, in her opinion, such law is unconstitutional, is a direct usurpation on the just powers of the general government, and on the equal rights of other States, a plain violation of the Constitution, and a proceeding essentially revolutionary in its character and tendency."

These four propositions having thus been plainly stated, Webster plunged into a long and careful argument in support of them. The bursts of rhetoric, the sarcasm, the personal allusions, the dramatic episodes which marked his two replies to Hayne, were wanting. The speech was such as might well have been addressed to the Supreme Court, and was without doubt but an elaboration of the letter he had intended to address to Chancellor Kent in reply to the letter of Calhoun to Governor Hamilton. That concessions of some kind must be made to South Carolina was generally admitted in both houses of Congress, and a bill to accomplish this end was reported to the House at the close of December. The existing tariff was to be swept away, duties were to be brought down to the rates of the tariff of 1816, and, as the members of Congress well knew, the bill was an administration measure. But in February, while the House was toiling earnestly to come to an agreement on the bill before the session should close on the 4th of March, Clay, to the amazement of his friends, brought before the Senate a compromise bill of his own. As passed,—for pass it did,—the act provided that all existing duties should be reduced to an ad valorem basis; that such as exceeded twenty per cent. should be so reduced that the excess should be diminished one tenth on September 30, 1833, and one tenth on September 30, 1835, 1837, and 1839; that one half of the remainder should be removed on September 30, 1841, and another half in 1842, when there would thus be established a horizontal tariff of twenty per cent. ad valorem on all dutiable goods. The free list was much increased, the credit system was abolished, all duties were to be paid in cash, and valuation at the port of entry was required. Such a bill from such a man; such duties from "the father of the American System," the champion of protection, took the country by surprise. "Mr. Clay's new tariff project," said one advocate of protection, "will be received like a crash of thunder in the winter season, and some will hardly trust the evidence of their senses on a first examination of it, so radical and sudden is the change of policy proposed."

So astonished was the Senate that the bill was

not allowed to go to a committee, but was merely ordered to be printed. This delay afforded Webster time to express his dissent in a set of resolutions. In substance they were that the annual revenue of the country ought not to be allowed to exceed the needs of the government; that as soon as it was certain that the duties imposed by the tariff act of 1832 would yield an excess of revenue they ought to be reduced; that in making this reduction it was not wise to proceed by way of an equal reduction per centum on all articles; but that the amount as well as the time ought to be fixed in respect to the several articles distinctly, having due regard to the questions how far such reduction would affect revenue, how far those domestic manufactures hitherto protected, and how far the rate of wages and the earnings of the American workingman; that it was unwise and injudicious, in laying import dues, to limit all dues to one equal rate per centum, and that since all power to protect home manufactures by commercial regulations or import duties had been taken from the States and given to the Congress of the United States, no law ought to be passed giving any pledge, express or implied, or giving any assurance, direct or indirect, tending to restrain Congress from at any time giving reasonable protection to American industry.

Having presented his resolutions, Webster expressed a wish to say something in their defense, but yielded in order that the debate on the Revenue

WEBSTER'S HOUSE IN SUMMER ST., BOSTON.

Collection Bill might be continued. What he said later was brief, of little importance, and soon forgotten. But the reply to Calhoun was not forgotten. It was hailed with delight by every lover of the Union, raised Webster still higher in popular esteem, and pleased no one so much as Jackson. Writing to his friend Poinsett the day after its delivery, the President said: "Mr. Webster replied to Calhoun yesterday, and, it is said, demolished him. It is believed by more than one that Mr. C. is in a state of dementation; his speech was a perfect failure, and Mr. Webster handled him like a child." He was thanked by the President personally, praised by the Secretary of State, and when, in the summer of 1833, he set off on a pleasure trip to the West, his journey was one long ovation. Everywhere he was welcomed as "the champion of the Constitution." That actual nullification by a State of an act of Congress should be met firmly and, if need be, put down by force was generally approved. But it was equally necessary that the meaning of the Constitution should be made quite plain, that the doctrine of nullification should be refuted, that the right to use force should be upheld; and this service Webster, in the opinion of his countrymen, had rendered in a most signal manner. At Utica the citizens forgot political differences in their eagerness to meet him. At Buffalo a public dinner was tendered, an address was delivered by the merchants and manufacturers;

and some months later he received from the mechanics of the town a fine black-walnut table as a token of appreciation. He was present at the launching of a steamboat bearing his name, and went in her to Cleveland, where he turned southward.

At Columbus another dinner was declined, but at Cincinnati he was forced to accept a like invitation, and was toasted as "The Daniel of his age —He may be cast among lions, as many as you please, but even then you will find him the master spirit"; as he "Who yesterday came among a community of strangers, and to-morrow leaves a community of friends"; as "The profound expounder of the Constitution, the eloquent supporter of the Federal Union, and the uniform friend and advocate of the Western country." More invitations to visit the neighboring State now came to him; but he turned eastward, and was dined and toasted at Washington and Pittsburg. As he drew near the latter town, he was met by the mayor and a body of citizens on horseback and escorted to the Exchange Hotel, which, says a contemporary account, "has been thronged ever since by crowds of eager visitors, without regard to party, anxious to see and testify respect to him whom all unite in regarding as an intellectual giant on whom the Constitution itself did not disdain to lean at a moment of imminent peril. Agreeable to previous arrangement, he was waited on by a committee of forty of our most respectable citizens to welcome him to Pittsburg, to proffer facilities for seeing to advantage whatever he might deem worthy of examination, and invite him to a public dinner." This being declined, "the idea of a formal dinner was abandoned; but as the anxiety seemed intense for some collective expression of public admiration, it was decided to invite him to meet our citizens at the spacious grove of Mr. Miltenberger on Monday afternoon at four o'clock. The change of plan was judicious, and the scene a truly gratifying one. Refreshments of a plain kind were spread around, in charge of the committee, but the tables could serve only as a nucleus to the vast multitude. Mr. Webster moved freely about the beautiful grounds, recognizing his numerous visitors of the preceding days, who were led, by the frank and engaging cordiality of his manners, to become, in turn, the introducers of such as had not before enjoyed the pleasure of taking him by the hand."

The speech on this occasion was another eulogy of the Constitution and the Union, another denunciation of the needlessness and folly of nullification, and a defense of the proclamation and the Force Act. The mayor in introducing him, he said, had done more than justice to his efforts, but had not overstated the occasion on which those efforts were made. "Gentlemen, it is but a few short months since dark and portentous clouds did hang over the heavens, and did shut out, as it were, the sun in his glory. A new and perilous crisis was upon us. . . . Gentlemen, this was an alarming moment. In common with all good citizens, I felt it to be such. A general anxiety pervaded the breasts of all who were, at home, partaking in the prosperity, honor, and happiness which the country had enjoyed. And how was it abroad? Why, gentlemen, every intelligent friend of human liberty, throughout the world, looked with amazement at the spectacle which we exhibited. In a day of unparalleled prosperity, after a half-century's most happy experience of the blessings of our Union, when we had already become the wonder of all the liberal part of the world and the envy of the illiberal, when the Constitution had so amply falsified the predictions of its enemies, and more than fulfilled the hopes of its friends; in a time of peace, with an overflowing treasury; when both the population and the improvement of the country had outrun the most sanguine anticipation; it was at this moment that we showed ourselves to the whole civilized world as being apparently on the eve of disunion and anarchy, at the very point of dissolving once and forever that Union which had made us so prosperous and so great. It was at this moment that those appeared among us who seemed ready to break up the national Constitution, and to scatter the twenty-four States into twenty-four unconnected communities. . . .

"Gentlemen, I hope that the result of that experiment may prove salutary in its consequences to our government, and so to the interests of the community. I hope that the signal and decisive manifestation of public opinion which has, for the time at least, put down the despotism of nullification, may produce permanent good effect. I know full well that popular topics may be urged against the proclamation. I know that it may be said, in regard to the laws of last session, that if such laws are to be maintained, Congress may pass what laws they please and enforce them. But may it not be said, on the other hand, that if a State may nullify one law, she may nullify any other law also, and, therefore, that the principle strikes at the whole power of Congress? Those who argue against the power of Congress, from the possibility of its abuse, entirely forget that if the power of State interposition be allowed, that power may be abused also. What is more material, they forget the will of the people as they have plainly expressed it in the Constitution. They forget that *the people have chosen* to give Congress a power of legislation independent of State control. They forget that the Confederation has ceased, and that a *Constitution*, a *government*, has taken its place."

At New York a serious effort was made to attach him to Jackson. This was not possible, for when Congress met the struggle with Jacksonism began, and through it all Webster sided with the Whigs.

13

CHAPTER X

THE reëlection of Jackson in the autumn of 1832 was construed by him to mean a popular indorsement of his financial policy, of his hostility to the Bank of the United States, and of his veto of the bill to renew its charter. In his own words, "The bank came into Congress and asked a new charter. The object avowed by many of the advocates of the bank was to put the President to the test, that the country might know his final determination relative to the bank prior to the ensuing election. . . . Can it now be said that the question of a recharter of the bank was not decided at the election which ensued? . . . Whatever may be the opinion of others, the President considers his reëlection as a decision of the people against the bank. . . . He was sustained by a just people, and he desires to evince his gratitude by carrying into effect their decision so far as it depends on him."

The best way to evince this gratitude was, to Jackson's mind, to go on with his warfare. And now that the charter could not be renewed, the best way to carry on the war was to attack the credit of the bank by removing the government deposits. Bent on this, the President assembled his cabinet one day in September, announced to it his determination, and read a long paper in which were set forth his reasons for the act. But the order to the receivers of public money to make no more deposits in the bank or its branches must be issued by the Secretary of the Treasury. The secretary was William J. Duane, who stoutly refused to disturb the deposits, and for this resistance to the will of Jackson he was promptly removed, and his office bestowed on Roger B. Taney.

Then the order was given, twenty-three "pet banks" were chosen to be the keepers of public money, and the whole country was instantly thrown into commotion.

In the Senate, where the enemies of Jackson were in the majority, the war against him was waged vigorously. First came a resolution calling on the President for a copy of the paper said to have been read to the cabinet. This was refused, and the right of the Senate to ask for the paper was flatly denied. Next came the resolutions containing the famous censure of Jackson; and while these were under consideration, memorials, petitions, resolutions poured into Congress by hundreds. No act ever done by any President since the days of Washington so excited the people. Party feeling was allayed, and Whigs, anti-Masons, and Jackson men united in the common shout of condemnation.

The legislatures of eight States approved, and the legislatures of eight denounced the conduct of the President. From congressional districts, counties, cities, towns, banks, chambers of commerce, boards of trade, merchants, traders, farmers, artizans of all sorts, came petitions bearing hundreds of signatures, and picturing the distress caused by the ruin of credit and confidence and the disorder of the currency. Laborers, it was said, had been thrown out of employment, mills and factories were closed, buying and selling almost ceased, and all because of a needless attack on the business interests of the people. Some of the petitioners prayed for a renewal of the bank charter; others for a restoration of the deposits; others upheld the President, opposed a new bank, and asked that the deposits be not returned.

Into the struggle thus begun Webster entered with an ardor he never before displayed. He gave his support and vote to Clay's resolutions of censure on the President, wrote the report of the committee condemning the reasons of the secretary for obeying the order of Jackson, and, before the session closed, attacked the financial policy of the administration scores of times in speeches long and short, some of which still find a place in his collected works. That on "A Redeemable Paper Currency" and that on "The Natural Hatred of the Poor to the Rich" may be read with profit to-day.

The vote of censure having passed the Senate, and having been entered on the "Journal," the President prepared a long message and protest, which he sent to the Senate in April, 1834, with the request that it also might be entered at length on the "Journal." Webster was then away on leave, but, hearing at Philadelphia that a protest had been presented, he started at once for Washington. It was Sunday morning when the steamboat reached Baltimore, and "It had been given out," says the account, "that they [Webster and Mr. Horace Binney] would not come that day, perhaps to prevent the gathering of a crowd; but the people by thousands assembled on the wharf. Mr. Webster, being called on, made a few animated remarks from the boat, with a view of dismissing the 'Friends of the Constitution' assembled to meet him. But they would not be dismissed. They formed into a solid body, filling the whole street, and marched up to the City Hotel. When he arrived at the hotel, hardly less than five thousand well-dressed persons, very many of them elderly men and of lofty standing in society, were assembled in front of it, and the gentlemen were successively called on to offer a few words of exhortation. The people were highly excited, and often cheered, but in a subdued tone of voice." For this Senator Forsyth denounced him as having addressed a "bawling crowd" on the Sabbath, as having excited a "wretched clamor," and as having "designs to exasperate the people to treasonable acts unless they submitted to the power of a great moneyed corporation.''

The speech which Webster hurried to Washington to make against the protest is a careful examination of the powers and duties of the Executive, and of the powers and duties of the Senate, and a fine example of that clearness of statement and of argument in which he was unrivaled.

Activity of this sort added to his renown, brought down on him the wrath of the friends of Jackson, and greatly increased the admiration felt for him by all who about this time began to call themselves Whigs. The cartoonists now attacked him as a national character. In one of their pictures a fountain of Congress water has exploded, and as Clay and Webster are blown into the air the latter exclaims, ''Thus vaulting ambition doth o'erleap itself and falls on t' other side.'' In another Jackson holds in his hand the order for the removal of the deposits. The lightning from the paper is demolishing the bank, and Clay, who has fallen amid the tottering columns, cries out, ''Help me up, Webster, or I shall lose my stakes!'' To this appeal Webster answers as he runs away: '' 'There is a tide in the affairs of men,' as Shakspere says. Sorry, dear Clay. Look out for yourself.'' In yet another cartoon ''Old Hickory'' and ''Bully Nick'' are about to engage in a ''set-to,'' with ''Long Harry'' and ''Black Dan'' as seconds to the Bully.

Again, Webster, as a cat mounted on a copy of the Constitution placed upon a chair, is worried by the dog Benton, standing on the floor.

During the summer of 1835, business having taken Webster to Bangor, he accepted a dinner; but so many people wished to hear and see him that, when the cloth was removed, he was forced to make his speech from the balcony of the hotel. Again his theme was the Constitution, which appeared, he said, to have been formed for two grand purposes. "The first is the union of the States. It is the bond of that union, and it states and defines its terms. . . . For one, I am not sanguine enough to believe that if this bond of union were dissolved, any other tie uniting all the States would take its place for generations to come. It requires no common skill, it is no ordinary piece of political journey-work to form a system which shall hold together four-and-twenty separate State sovereignties, the line of whose united territories runs down all the parallels of latitude from New Brunswick to the Gulf of Mexico, and whose connected breadth stretches from the sea far beyond the Mississippi. Nor are all times or all occasions suited to such great operations. . . . Whoever, therefore, undervalues this National Union, whoever depreciates it, whoever accustoms us to consider how the people might get on without it, appears to me to encourage sentiments subversive of the foundation of our prosperity. . . .

"Another object of the Constitution I take to be such as is common to all written constitutions of free governments—that is, to fix limits to delegated authority, or, in other words, to impose constitutional restraints on political power. . . . It is not among the circumstances of the times most ominous for good, that a diminished estimate appears to be placed on those constitutional securities. A disposition is but too prevalent to substitute personal confidence for legal restraint—to put trust in men, rather than in principles. . . . Whatever government is not a government of law is a despotism, let it be called what it may."

A few weeks later, when a silver vase was presented to "the defender of the Constitution" at Boston, Webster spoke more plainly still of this change in the Constitution. "I think, then, gentlemen, that a great practical change is going on in the Constitution, which, if not checked, must completely alter its whole character. This change consists in the diminution of the just powers of Congress on the one hand, and in the vast increase of executive authority on the other. The government of the United States in the aggregate, or the legislative power of Congress, seems fast losing, one after another, its accustomed powers. One by one they are practically struck out of the Constitution. What has become of the power of internal improvement? Does it remain in the Constitution, or is it erased by the repeated exercise of the Presi-

CAROLINE LEROY, MR. WEBSTER'S SECOND WIFE.

dent's veto, and the acquiescence in that exercise of all who call themselves his friends, whatever their opinions of the Constitution? The power to create a national bank,— . . . is it not true that party has agreed to strike this power, too, from the Constitution in compliance with what has been openly called the interests of party? Nay, more; that great power, the power of protecting domestic industry, who can tell me whether that power is now regarded as in the Constitution or out of it?''

Webster's name now began to be seriously mentioned as that of the next Whig candidate for the Presidency. Indeed, the Whigs in the Massachusetts legislature formally nominated him, and letters promising support came to him from Vermont, New York, Ohio, and Louisiana. His nomination was indorsed by the Whigs of Penobscot County, Maine, and by his party in Berwyn, Hallowell, and Portland. Webster delegates to the Pennsylvania State Convention were chosen in the counties of Chester and Allegheny, and some questions were asked him by the anti-Masonic State Committee. But the Whigs agreed on William Henry Harrison as the more available man, and nominated him.

For Webster to remain longer in the field as a serious candidate was useless, and when, in March, 1836, a convention of Whig members of the Massachusetts legislature and delegates from towns not represented by Whigs in the General Court gathered in Boston, he wrote expressing a desire to withdraw. But the convention would not hear of such a thing, voted that he was the true Whig candidate, and at the autumn election Massachusetts cast her fourteen electoral votes for Daniel Webster. He received no others, but had no cause for regret, for the Whigs were overwhelmingly beaten, and Van Buren succeeded Jackson.

The success of Van Buren was disheartening, and for many reasons Webster now thought seriously of retiring from the Senate. While a member of the House and but one in a State delegation of twelve, he had found it an easy matter to carry on a lucrative practice in the Supreme Court. The interests of his State were then safe in the care of many colleagues. But as a senator he was one of two, and duty to his country and to his State left little time for practice, and his income went down rapidly. The fight with nullification in 1833 cut down his professional gains by eight thousand dollars, and never since had his earnings approached what they might have been. A longing for a great Western farm had seized him, and he had already acquired a little tract not far from Springfield, Ohio, which he named Salisbury, after the old home of his father. This he hoped to enlarge. He would make it a tract of a thousand acres and engage in farming on a great scale. All this required money, and money was not to be made by attendance in the Senate. In January, 1837, therefore, he wrote to friends in Massachusetts, announcing his wish to resign, and urging that the legislature at once elect a successor. But as news of his intention spread, Whigs in all quarters besought him not to withdraw. Those in the Massachusetts legislature strongly opposed the step, and appointed a committee, with the Speaker, Robert C. Winthrop, at their head, to beseech him to remain in the Senate, or at least to postpone his resignation. At New York city a meeting of his political friends was called, Chancellor Kent placed in the chair, and an invitation to a public reception tendered. If he must leave the Senate, this was to be a testimonial of a lively sense of his public services. If he could be persuaded to remain, it was to be an opportunity to express their wishes to him in a manner as impressive as possible. He did consent to remain, accepted the New York invitation, and one day in March, 1837, was met at Amboy by a committee, and escorted to Niblo's Garden, where, in the presence of a vast throng, he gave utterance to his "sentiments freely on the great topics of the day" in what was long remembered as the "Niblo's Garden Speech."

Again his theme was the Union and the Constitution. "The general government," said he, "to the extent of its power is national. It is not consolidated, it does not embrace all the powers of government. On the contrary, it is delegated, restrained, strictly limited. But what power it does possess, it possesses for the general, not for any partial or local, good. It extends over a vast territory, embracing now six-and-twenty States, with interests various but not irreconcilable, infinitely diversified but capable of being all blended into political harmony. He, however, who would produce this harmony must survey the whole field. . . . We are one in respect to the glorious Constitution under which we live. We are all united in the great brotherhood of American liberty. Descending from the same ancestors, bred in the same school, taught in infancy to imbibe the same general political sentiments, Americans all, by birth, education, and principle, what but a narrow mind or woeful ignorance or prejudice ten times blinded can lead any of us to regard the citizens of any part of the country as strangers and aliens?

"Under the present Constitution, wisely administered, all are safe, happy, and renowned. . . . But if the system is broken, its fragments must fall alike on all. Not only the cause of American liberty, but the grand cause of liberty throughout the whole earth, depends in a great measure on upholding the Constitution and Union of these States. If shattered and destroyed, no matter by what cause, the peculiar and cherished idea of United American Liberty will be no more forever. There may be free States, it is possible, when there shall be separate States. There may be many loose and feeble and hostile confederacies where there is now one great and united confederacy. But the noble idea of United American Liberty, of *our* liberty, such as our fathers established it, will be extinguished forever. . . . Let us, then, stand by the Constitution as it is, and by our country as it is—one, united, and entire; let it be a truth engraven on our hearts, let it be borne on the flag under which we rally in every exigency, that we have ONE COUNTRY, ONE CONSTITUTION, ONE DESTINY.''

In the spring of 1837 Webster again determined to visit the West, and in May was on his way to the Ohio. As he went down the river, a steamboat bearing a hundred citizens of Wheeling met and escorted him to their town, where a throng awaited him at the landing. A dinner and a speech followed. At Maysville multitudes from the country round about came to see and greet him. At Lexington there was another public dinner, and at Louisville a barbecue, at which he again spoke for two hours. Thence he went on to North Bend to visit General Harrison, and to Cincinnati, where there was another outpouring of the people and another speech. At St. Louis he was greeted, said a newspaper, as no other citizen was ever received on the west bank of the Mississippi. At Alton, across the river, flags were displayed, the church bells rang, and cannon fired as he came ashore. The great panic of 1837 was now sweeping over the country, Van Buren had summoned Congress to a special session, and at Madison Webster turned homeward. As he drew near Chicago, a long train of wagons and horsemen met him ten miles from the town, escorted him to the Lake House, where he spoke to the crowd that packed the street. The next day he attended a festival held in his honor. Pushing eastward, he visited Michigan City, Toledo, and Buffalo, where he was entertained with a steamboat regatta on the lake, and then went on to New York and Boston.

CHAPTER XI

THE decision of Webster to remain in the Senate brought him to another turning-point in his political career, and he went back to begin a new contest with Calhoun for the preservation of the Union. The first struggle arose over the tariff, and ended in nullification. The second began over slavery, and led to secession. Mr. Benton is authority for the statement that when Calhoun went back to his home in the spring of 1833, disappointed and downhearted at the slight support the South had given to the act of nullification, he told his friends that the South could never be united against the North on the question of the tariff, and that the basis of Southern union must henceforth be the questions that sprang from slavery. Certain it is that by 1833 the work of the abolitionists and antislavery people began to tell. It was in 1831 that the first number of the "Liberator" appeared, and the State of Georgia offered five thousand dollars to any one who would kidnap Garrison and bring him to the State. It was in 1833 that the American Antislavery Society was founded, and the "Telegraph," a nullification journal published at Washington, flatly charged the people of the North with a deliberate purpose to destroy slavery in the South. Twenty newspapers in twenty different parts of the North and the South at once made answer, denying the charge, and accusing Calhoun and the nullifiers of again attempting to wreck the Union. "His object," said one, "is to fan the flame of discord and separate the South from the North. Mr. Calhoun has been defeated in his ambitious project of reaching the Presidency. He would now gladly ruin the fair fabric of the United States that he might become the chief of a Southern confederacy. The tariff was to have been the pretext for separation. This having failed, a new cause is sought in the question of slavery, and such miserable fanatics as Garrison and wretched publications as the 'Liberator' are quoted as evidence of the feeling of the people of the North."

But the movement thus started would not go down. In 1834 there were antislavery riots in New York and Philadelphia. It was in 1835 that Garrison was mobbed in Boston; that there was a riot in Utica; that antislavery papers were taken from the post-office in Charleston, South Carolina, and burned on the public square; that Jackson in his message asked for the exclusion of such documents from the mails; and that four slaveholding States requested the non-slaveholding to suppress the abolitionists. It was in 1836 that James G. Birney was mobbed in Cincinnati; that Calhoun presented a bill to stop the delivery by postmasters of antislavery books, papers, tracts, and pictures; and that the House of Representatives passed the first of the gag resolutions. It was in 1837, a few weeks before Webster spoke in Niblo's Garden, that the United States recognized the independence of the slaveholding republic of Texas.

The fate of slavery was now clearly a national issue, and in the Niblo's Garden speech Webster placed himself on record. That a desire or intention to annex Texas to the United States already existed could not be disguised, he said. To this he saw objections, insurmountable objections.

"When the Constitution was formed it is not probable," said he, "that either its framers or the people ever looked to the admission of any States into the Union, except such as then already existed and such as should be formed out of territory then already belonging to the United States. Fifteen years after the adoption of the Constitution, however, the case of Louisiana arose. Louisiana was obtained by treaty with France, who had recently obtained it from Spain, but the object of this acquisition certainly was not mere extension of territory. Other great political interests were connected with it. Spain, while she possessed Louisiana, had held the mouth of the great rivers which rise in the Western States and flow into the Gulf of Mexico. She had disputed our use of the rivers. . . . The command of these rivers to the sea

14

was, therefore, the great object arrived at in the acquisition of Louisiana.''

A like policy and a like necessity led to the purchase of Florida. But no such policy required the annexation of Texas. Her addition to our territory was not necessary to the full and complete enjoyment of that already possessed. The limits of the Union in that direction ought not to be extended. Texas, moreover, was likely to be a slaveholding country, no matter by whom possessed, and he was not willing to do anything that should ''extend the slavery of the African race on this continent, or add other slaveholding States to the Union. . . . When I say that I regard slavery in itself as a great moral, social, and political evil, I only use language which has been adopted by distinguished men, themselves citizens of slaveholding States. I shall do nothing, therefore, to favor or encourage its further extension. We have slavery already amongst us. The Constitution found it in the Union; it recognized it, and gave it solemn guarantees. To the full extent of these guarantees we are all bound in honor, in justice, and by the Constitution. . . . But when we come to speak of admitting new States, the subject assumes an entirely different aspect. Our rights and our duties are then both different. . . . When it is proposed to bring new members into this political partnership, the old members have a right to say under what terms such new partners are to come

in, and what they are to bring along with them.
. . . In my opinion, the people of the United
States will not consent to bring into the Union
a new, vastly extensive, and slaveholding country, large enough for half a dozen or a dozen
States. In my opinion, they ought not to consent
to it." Here was free-soilism plainly stated, and
here, as Webster claimed thirteen years later, was
to be found the principle of the Wilmot Proviso.

As he was not a Southern expansionist, so he
was not a Northern abolitionist. "Slavery as it
exists in the States," said he, "is beyond the reach
of Congress. It is a concern of the States themselves. They have never submitted it to Congress,
and Congress has no rightful power over it. I
shall concur, therefore, in no act, no measure, no
menace, no indication of purpose which shall interfere, or threaten to interfere, with the exclusive
authority of the several States over the subject of
slavery as it exists within their respective limits.
All this appears to me to be matter of plain and
imperative duty."

On the great question then before Congress—the
right of citizens to petition for the abolition of
slavery in the District of Columbia, and the duty
of Congress to receive and its power to grant petitions—he said not a word. Yet there was no phase
of the struggle for the rights of man which at that
time more deeply interested the people. For nearly
a decade past the abolitionists had been flooding

the Senate and the House at each session with petitions to abolish both slavery and the slave-trade in the District over which Congress had absolute jurisdiction. So long as the pro-slavery party was content to allow these petitions to take the usual course of such appeals, so long as it would suffer them to be received, committed, and utterly forgotten, no serious consequences followed. But their increasing number, the persistence with which they were introduced, the spirit believed to animate their signers, and fear of the evils likely to follow a constant agitation of the slavery question had, of late years, so alarmed the slaveholders that in 1836 the House of Representatives ordered that every paper which in any way had to do with slavery should, without being printed or referred, be laid upon the table, and that no further action whatever should be had thereon. As yet the Senate was not ready to go so far; but when, in December, 1837, Calhoun presented resolutions on the subject of slavery, and Clay moved a substitute for one of them, Webster spoke out. "The intermeddling," said Calhoun, "of any State, or States, or their citizens, to abolish slavery in this District, or any of the territories, on the ground or under the pretext that it is immoral or sinful, or the passage of any act or measure of Congress with that view, would be a direct and dangerous attack on the institutions of all the slave States." Such interference, said Clay, "would be a violation of the faith implied in the

cession by the States of Virginia and Maryland.''
From this Webster dissented. He denied that any
faith had been plighted, maintained the absolute
jurisdiction of Congress over the District, and held
that there was nothing in the act of cession, nothing in the Constitution, nothing in the whole history of the transaction, implying any limitation on
the right of Congress to legislate as it pleased on
slavery. ''If,'' said he, ''the assertion contained
in this resolution be true, a very strange result, as
it seems to me, must follow. The resolution affirms
that the faith of Congress is plighted indefinitely.
If this be so, then it is an obligation that binds us
forever, as much as if it were one of the prohibi-
tions of the Constitution itself. And at all times
hereafter, even if, in the course of their history,
availing themselves of events, or changing their
views of policy, the States themselves should make
provision for the emancipation of their slaves, the
existing state of things could not be changed, nevertheless, in this District. It does really seem to me
that if this resolution, in its terms, be true, though
slavery in every other part of the world may be
abolished, yet in the metropolis of this great republic it is established in perpetuity.''

Whether slavery was or was not abolished concerned him little. The constitutional question alone
interested him, and, writing of the resolutions to
a friend, he said: ''Mr. Clay and Mr. Calhoun
have attempted in 1838 what, in my judgment, they

attempted in 1833—to make a new Constitution.''
Nor was this a hasty judgment. That Calhoun was
really bent on some scheme harmful to the Constitution and the Union seems to have been Webster's
deliberate belief; and later in the session of 1838,
in a speech famous in its day, he reviewed the political conduct of Calhoun since 1833, and charged him
with a steady design to break up the Union. ''The
honorable member from South Carolina,'' said he,
''habitually indulges in charges of usurpation and
oppression against the government of his country.
He daily denounces its important measures in the
language in which our Revolutionary fathers spoke
of the oppression of the mother country. . . .
A principal object in his late political movements,
the gentleman himself tells us, was to unite the
entire South; and against whom or against what
does he wish to unite the entire South? . . .
While the gentleman thus wishes to unite the entire
South, I pray to know, sir, if he expects me to turn
toward the polar star, and, acting on the same principle, to utter a cry of Rally! to the whole North?
Heaven forbid! To the day of my death neither
he nor others shall ever hear such a cry from me.

''Finally, the honorable member declares that
he shall now march off under the banner of State
Rights! March off from whom? March off from
what? We have been contending for great principles. We have been struggling to maintain the
liberty and to restore the prosperity of the coun-

try; we have made these struggles here, in the national councils, with the old flag, the true American flag, the eagle and the stars and stripes, waving over the chamber in which we sit. He now tells us, however, that he marches off under the States' Rights banner.

"Let him go. I remain. I am where I ever have been and ever mean to be. Here, standing on the platform of the general Constitution,—a platform broad enough and firm enough to uphold every interest of the whole country,—I shall still be found. . . . I move off under no banner not known to the whole American people, and to their Constitution and laws."

The position thus publicly taken by Webster on the annexation of Texas, the abolition of slavery, and the power of Congress to make the District of Columbia free soil, brought out letters asking for further statements of his opinion on the question of the hour. To one he wrote: "I think you would be very safe in adopting, in your House, an anti-Texas report. As to slavery, I think it very safe to adopt a resolution condemning Mr. Patton's resolution. Whether it will be best to go farther, you who are on the spot can best decide. My own opinion is that the antislavery feeling is growing stronger and stronger every day; and while we must be careful to countenance nothing which violates the Constitution or invades the rights of others, it is our policy, in my opinion most clearly, not to yield the substantial truth for the sake of conciliating those whom we never can conciliate, at the expense of the loss of the friendship and support of those great masses of good men who are interested in the antislavery cause.

"I send you inclosed a copy of a letter lately addressed by me to Mr. Peck of the House of Representatives. It states shortly the opinions which I hold, and am ready to express, on the general slavery question. I refer you also to some remarks of mine, published in the 'Intelligencer,' upon Mr. Clay's substitute for Mr. Calhoun's resolution."

In this letter to Mr. Peck, Webster declares his belief to be that Congress has no power to free slaves in any State, but may do so in the District of Columbia, and may regulate the purchase and sale of slaves in the District in any manner thought just and expedient; that the citizens of the United States may petition for the abolition of slavery in the District; and "that all such petitions, being respectfully written, ought to be received, read, referred, and considered in the same manner as petitions on other important subjects."

The campaign of 1840 was now at hand, and as all signs pointed to a great Whig victory, the Whigs of Massachusetts put Webster in nomination. But no one else thought of him for a moment, and when the National Convention met in December, 1839, William Henry Harrison was chosen to lead the party. No platform was adopted, but a

Baltimore newspaper furnished one in the sneer
that, with two thousand dollars a year, Harrison
would be content to live in a log cabin and drink
hard cider, and this was all the Whigs needed. To
discuss issues and principles was useless. As Webster said truly, the people wanted a change, and a
change they were determined to have, and for a
party bent on a change the Hero of Tippecanoe was
just the man and the slur cast on his poverty was
just the platform. Save the little red school-house,
nothing was dearer to the heart of the people than
the log cabin, and no insult more galling could possibly have been uttered. That humble abode, with
its puncheon floor, its mud-smeared sides, its latch-
string, its window, where well-greased paper did
duty for glass, had ever been, and was still, the
symbol of American hardihood, and instantly became the true Whig watchword. On vacant lots
in every city and town, on ten thousand village
greens, the cabin, with a coon's skin on the wall,
with the latch-string hanging out in token of welcome, and with a barrel of hard cider close beside
the door, became the Whig headquarters. Mounted
on wheels and occupied by speakers, it was dragged
from village to village. Log-cabin raisings, log-
cabin medals, log-cabin badges, magazines, alma-
nacs, song-books, pictures, were everywhere to be
seen; and into this wild campaign of song and
laughter Webster entered with unwonted zeal.
Though nobody wanted him to be President, the

whole country seemed possessed to hear him speak. Countless Tippecanoe clubs elected him a member; innumerable "raisings" claimed his presence. New Hampshire appealed to him as the State where he was born. The West clamored for him as the stanch friend of her interests. A score of towns wanted him as the orator for the Fourth of July. The candidate himself was not so eagerly sought.

To many of their appeals Webster acceded, and addressed meeting after meeting till, he writes to his wife, he is "sore from speaking." In another letter he tells her: "I am charged with burning the convent at Charlestown [1836]. Do you recollect how I did it? Will you promise not to betray me if I deny it?"

His great speeches were at Saratoga, Bunker Hill, New York, and Richmond. At Saratoga, catching the spirit of the times, he lamented that he too had not been born in a log cabin. "Gentlemen, it did not happen to me to be born in a log cabin; but my elder brothers and sisters were born in a log cabin, raised amid the snow-drifts of New Hampshire at a period so early that when the smoke first rose from its rude chimney and curled over the frozen hills there was no similar evidence of a white man's habitation between it and the settlements on the rivers of Canada. Its remains still exist. I make to it an annual visit. I carry my children to it, to teach them the hardships endured by the generations which have gone before them.

. . . And if ever I am ashamed of it, or if I ever fail in affectionate veneration for him who raised it, and defended it against savage violence and destruction, cherished all the domestic virtues beneath its roof, and, through the fire and blood of a seven years' revolutionary war, shrank from no danger, no toil, no sacrifice, to serve his country, and to raise his children to a condition better than his own, may my name and the name of my posterity be blotted forever from the memory of mankind!'' After the Bunker Hill festival, the area covered by the crowd was measured, and seventy-five thousand persons were said to have attended.

At Richmond, in October, Webster spoke to the Whig Convention gathered in the Capitol Square to do him honor. He stood now on dangerous ground, for the cry had been raised that to invite such a man to come to Virginia and speak to Virginians was a great breach of propriety. That he should make clear his views on certain matters seemed to him therefore quite necessary; and as one of these was slavery, he took occasion, in the course of the speech, to put himself again on record. ''I am brought,'' said he, ''to advert for one moment to what I constantly see in all the administration papers from Baltimore south. It is one perpetual outcry, admonishing the people of the South that their own State governments, and the property they hold under them, are not secure if

they admit a Northern man to any considerable
share in the administration of the general government. You all know that that is the universal
cry. . . . I shall ask some friend connected
with the press to circulate in Virginia what I said
on this subject in the Senate of the United States
in January, 1830. I have nothing to add to or sub-
tract from what I then said. I commend it to
your attention, or rather I desire you to look at
it. I hold that Congress is absolutely precluded
from interfering in any manner, direct or indirect,
with this or with any other of the institutions of
the States.'' When the delegates heard this they
cheered him wildly, and one in the crowd cried out,
''We wish this could be heard from Maryland to
Louisiana, and we wish that the sentiment just expressed may be repeated.'' ''Repeat! Repeat!''
was now heard on every side. ''Well,'' said Webster, ''I repeat it, proclaim it on the wings of all
the winds, tell it to all your friends [cries of ''We
will! We will!''], tell it, I say, that, standing here
in the capital of Virginia, beneath an October sun,
in the midst of this assemblage, before the entire
country and upon all the responsibility which be-
longs to me, I say that there is no power, direct
or indirect, in Congress or the general government
to interfere in the slightest degree with the institutions of the South.''

CHAPTER XII

SECRETARY OF STATE

THE election over and won, Harrison tendered the Department of State to Clay, and, when he refused, asked Webster to choose between the State Department and the Treasury. To this Webster replied: "The question of accepting a seat in your cabinet, should it be tendered me, has naturally been the subject of my reflections and of consultations with friends. The result of these reflections and consultations has been that I should accept the office of Secretary of State, should it be offered to me under circumstances such as now exist."

The President-elect answered: "I entirely approve of your choice of the two tendered you"; and on March 4, Webster, having resigned his seat in the Senate, took up the duties of Secretary of State.

The first official duty laid upon him was the revision of the inaugural address, which the President-elect had prepared with much pains, and which abounded in that sort of classical knowledge so fashionable when Harrison was a lad. Roman history was freely drawn on, and the speech was sprinkled with references to Cæsar, the proconsuls, and the Roman knights. This was too much for the new secretary, and, after a long struggle, the President-elect agreed to leave out most of his warnings from the past. The story is told that when the work of revision was over and Webster reached his lodgings, the mistress of the house remarked that he looked tired, and asked if anything had happened. "You would think that something had happened if you knew what I have done," was the reply. "I have killed seventeen Roman proconsuls." But Cæsar and the Roman knights escaped, and still adorn the inaugural address.

One month after its delivery Harrison died, and the stormy administration of Tyler began. At the special session of Congress called by Harrison to correct the evils of Democratic rule, Tyler agreed to most of the measures of reform. He signed the bill repealing the subtreasury act, the bill to distribute the proceeds of the sales of public land, the bill to change the banking system of the District of Columbia, and the revenue bill; but he vetoed the charter for a "Fiscal Bank of the United States," and the Whigs at once brought in a bill to establish a "Fiscal Corporation." While the matter was still before Congress, members of that body consulted Webster as to the best course to pursue, and were given this advice:

"I should not volunteer my opinions to you in any matter respecting the discharge of your public

JOSEPH STORY, ASSOCIATE JUSTICE OF THE SUPREME COURT.

duties in another department of the government; but as you spoke last evening of the general policy of the Whigs, under the present posture of affairs, relative to the Bank Bill, I am willing to place you in full possession of my opinion on that subject.

"It is not necessary to go farther back into the history of the past than the introduction of the present measure into the House of Representatives. That introduction took place within two or three days after the President's disapproval of the former bill, and I have not the slightest doubt that it was honestly and fairly intended as a measure likely to meet the President's approbation. I do not believe that one in fifty of the Whigs had any sinister design whatever, if there was an individual who had such design. But I know that the President had been greatly troubled in regard to the former bill, being desirous, on one hand, to meet the wishes of his friends if he could, and, on the other, to do justice to his own opinions. Having returned this first bill, with objections, a new one was presented in the House, and appeared to be making rapid progress. I know the President regretted this, and wished that the whole subject might have been postponed. At the same time, I believe he was disposed to consider calmly and conscientiously whatever other measure might be presented to him.

"But, in the meantime, Mr. Botts's very extraordinary letter made its appearance. Mr. Botts is a

Whig of eminence and influence in our ranks. I need not recall to your mind the contents of the letter. It is enough to say that it purported that the Whigs designed to circumvent their own President, to 'head him,' as the expression was, to place him in a condition of embarrassment. From that moment I felt that it was the duty of the Whigs to forbear from pressing the Bank Bill further at the present time. I thought it was but just in them to give decisive proof that they entertained no such purpose as seemed to be imputed to them. And since there was reason to believe that the President would be glad of time for information and reflection before being called on to form an opinion on another plan for a bank—a plan somewhat new to the country—I thought his known wishes ought to be complied with. I think so still. I think this is a course just to the President and wise on behalf of the Whig party. A decision which ought, in my judgment, to be given to the intimation, from whatever quarter, of a disposition among the Whigs to embarrass the President. This is the main ground of my opinion, and such a rebuke, I think, would be found in the general resolution of the party to postpone further proceedings on the subject to the next session, now only a little more than three months off.

"The session has been fruitful of important acts. The wants of the treasury have been supplied, provisions have been made for fortification and for the navy, the repeal of the subtreasury has passed, the Bankrupt Bill, that great measure of justice and benevolence, has been carried through, and the Land Bill seems about to receive the approbation of Congress. In all these measures, forming a mass of legislation more important, I will venture to say, than all the proceedings of Congress for many years past, the President has cordially concurred.

"I agree that the currency question is, nevertheless, the great question before the country; but, considering what has already been accomplished in regard to other things, considering the differences of opinion which exist upon this remaining one, and considering, especially, that it is the duty of the Whigs effectually to repel and put down any supposition that they are endeavoring to put the President in a condition in which he must act under restraint or embarrassment, I am fully and entirely persuaded that the bank subject should be postponed to the next session."

The advice was disregarded; the Fiscal Corporation Bill went to the President and was vetoed, and four members of the cabinet resigned in a body. A fifth soon followed, and the great Whig leaders, in a formal manifesto, read John Tyler out of the party. Webster remained in the cabinet. For a moment he seems to have been in doubt just what to do, and in his uncertainty wrote post-haste to a friend in Boston, "Do the Whigs of Massachusetts think I ought to quit or ought

15

to stay?'' and asked the Massachusetts delegation to meet him in consultation. The advice of those gentlemen was not to quit; and three days later, Webster, in a letter to a newspaper, made known his reasons for remaining. He saw no cause for the sudden dissolution of the cabinet by the voluntary act of its members; he believed that some sort of institution to aid the financial operations of the government and to give the country a good currency and cheap exchanges was absolutely necessary, and that, to get it, there must be a union of Whig President, Whig Congress, and Whig people. Having decided to remain in the Cabinet, Webster became the champion of the President, and in unsigned notes to newspapers attacked his late colleagues.

"It is plain enough," he said in one such note, "that the ex-secretaries take the President at great disadvantage.

"They write him letters which they know he cannot answer, because the President of the United States cannot enter into such a correspondence.

"They use weapons, therefore, which they know he cannot use.

"In the next place, they undertake to state Cabinet conversations, which he regards as confidential, and to which he cannot refer without violating his own sense of propriety and dignity.

"Having thus placed the President in a position in which he cannot defend himself, they make war upon him; and this we suppose high-mindedness and 'chivalry.' ''

Back of all this were far weightier reasons which he could not publicly declare. Grave questions of long standing between Great Britain and the United States were pressing for a settlement, peaceably if possible, forcibly if necessary; for settled they must be. The north boundary of Maine, after fifty-eight years of discussion, was still undefined. The affair of the *Caroline*, and the assumption by Great Britain of all responsibility for the destruction of that steamboat, had aroused the whole frontier of New York; the arrest and trial of McLeod had thrown Great Britain into a passion; while her assertion of a right to search ships supposed to be engaged in the African slave-trade stirred up a question once made a cause of war. Could Webster bring about a peaceful settlement of these many sources of ill feeling and ill will between two nations which of all others ought to be friends, he would render to his country services of no common sort; and the belief that he could do much to accomplish such an end was the chief reason why his State delegation was opposed to his resigning the Secretaryship of State. Again, he was an Eastern man, and, in the opinion of the people of Maine, the boundary question would never be settled till a man born and bred among them took the dispute in hand.

The first of these matters to be urged upon him was the case of Alexander McLeod. A rebellion which broke out in Canada in 1837 had with difficulty been put down; and toward the end of the year a band of Canadian refugees and American sympathizers took possession of Navy Island, set up a temporary government, adopted a flag and seal and issued paper money, and became an object of interest to all along the Niagara frontier. Seeing in this a chance to make a little money, the owner of a small steamboat called the *Caroline* cut her out of the ice in Buffalo Creek, and on the 29th of December, 1837, made two trips between Fort Schlosser and Navy Island, taking over men, arms, food, and a cannon. Sir Allan McNab, commander of the provincial forces, looked on this boat as in the service of the insurgents, called for volunteers to destroy her, and on the night of December 29 she was boarded at Fort Schlosser by five boat-loads of armed men, who drove her occupants ashore, gave her to the flames, and sent her, a blazing wreck, over Niagara Falls. In the course of the attack, several of our citizens were wounded, and one was killed outright. A formal demand for redress and apology was promptly made on the British government; but no apology was tendered, no redress was offered, and the affair was well-nigh forgotten when Alexander McLeod appeared at Lewiston one day in November, 1840, and boasted that he was one of the attacking party and had shot Amos Durfee. For this he was arrested on the charge of arson and murder and indicted by the grand jury in February, 1841. Meantime Mr. Fox, the British minister, who in 1838 treated the burning of the *Caroline* as the unauthorized act of private individuals, and described the *Caroline* as a boat of "piratical character," now demanded the instant release of McLeod, because the destruction of this steamboat was a public act of persons in his Majesty's service, obeying the orders of their superiors. Mr. Fox was then writing without authority. But in February Lord Palmerston assumed responsibility for the deed, declaring that "McLeod's execution would produce war—war immediate and frightful in its character, because it would be a war of retaliation and revenge"; and on March 12, 1841, Mr. Fox formally demanded McLeod's release in the name of Great Britain. The declaration that the invasion of our soil and the burning of the *Caroline* were acts authorized by Great Britain, the demand for the instant release of the prisoner, and the threat of war gave to the incident a serious character which Webster was not ready to meet. He put on a bold front, however, and then did all he could to secure the release of McLeod. The attorney-general was sent with all haste to New York with "authentic evidence of the recognition by the British government of the destruction of the *Caroline* as an act of public force, done by national authority." He was to "proceed to Lockport, or wherever else the trial may be holden, and furnish the prisoner's counsel with the evidence." He was to "see that he have skilful and eminent counsel, if such be not already retained"; and he was to say to them "that it is the wish of this government that, in case his defense be overruled by the court in which he shall be tried, proper steps be taken immediately for removing the cause, by writ of error, to the Supreme Court of the United States." A letter was then written to William H. Seward, Governor of New York.

"The President," said Webster, "has learned, not directly, but by means of a letter from a friend, that you had expressed a disposition to direct a *nolle prosequi* in the case of the indictment against McLeod, on being informed by this government that the British government had officially avowed the attack on the *Caroline* as an act done by its own authority.

"The President directs me to express his thanks for the promptitude with which you appear disposed to perform an act which he supposes proper for the occasion, and which is calculated to relieve this government from embarrassments and the country from some dangers of collision with a foreign power.

"You will have seen Mr. Crittenden, whom I take this occasion to commend to your kindest regard."

Governor Seward replied that he had "neither

expressed nor entertained the disposition to direct
a *nolle prosequi*" in the case of McLeod, but told
the attorney-general that he would pardon the prisoner if found guilty; that there should be no execution, no war.   Webster, however, was not content with such an answer.   Letters from Lewis
Cass, the American minister at Paris, assured him
that Great Britain was in earnest; that it was no
secret that her minister had been instructed to leave
Washington if McLeod was hanged; that the British fleet in the Mediterranean was to assemble grad-
ually at Gibraltar and sail thence to Halifax; and
that the English colony in Paris was heartily in
favor of war, which would be fought with great
bitterness.   That our own countrymen were quite
as ready was likewise no secret; for the report of
the Committee on Foreign Affairs, made in February, on the letters of Mr. Fox was far from
pacific, and during the debate on printing the report feeling ran high.   If war was to be averted,
the trial must be prevented; and, as one way to prevent it, Webster, in his reply to Mr. Fox, observed
that the indictment had been removed into the Supreme Court of New York, and that it was "now
competent for McLeod, by the ordinary process of
habeas corpus, to bring his case for hearing before
that tribunal."   The hint was taken; the writ was
sued out, and the first intimation Seward had of
this fact was when the prisoner passed through
Albany in charge of the sheriff to attend the sitting

of the court at New York.   Seward bade the attorney-general of New York resist the motion for the
discharge of McLeod.   The federal government
permitted the district attorney to act as one of the
counsel for McLeod, and the case was looked on
by the people as a struggle between the State and
federal governments.   At this stage the State triumphed, the discharge was refused, and the indictment was sent down to the Circuit Court, there to
be traversed.

Both President and secretary were greatly disappointed.   A speedy trial, if trial there must be,
was most desirable.   Every postponement, every
delay, meant a new cause of irritation to Great
Britain, raised the angry feelings of the people
along the border to a yet higher pitch, and made
the Hunters' Lodges and the Patriotic Societies
along the frontier from Maine to Wisconsin more
active than ever.   So grave did the danger from
this source seem that the secretary thought it well
worth while to investigate the doings of these clubs
by every means in his power.   An agent was sent
to confer with the army officers at Buffalo, Cleveland, and Detroit; the collectors, marshals, and district attorneys along the border were called on to
tell all they knew, and from these sources Webster
was soon able to advise the President what to do.
"I think," he wrote, "I have learned pretty fully
the real object and plan of open action of these
'Hunters' Lodges,' 'Patriotic Societies,' etc.,

which are in existence all along the northern frontier from Maine to Wisconsin.

"They are in constant correspondence with the disaffected in Canada, and these disaffected persons come over the line and harangue them in their secret meetings. They do not expect to be able to invade Canada with any hope of success unless war breaks out *between Canada and the United States; but they desire that event above all things,* and, to bring it about, will naturally join in any violence or outbreak if they think they can do so with impunity. They may even attempt violence upon McLeod, should he be discharged by the courts or on his way from the prison to the place where the court shall be sitting.

"The aggregate of the members of all these clubs is probably not less than ten thousand. Cleveland is rather their headquarters.

"If war breaks out, these persons do not propose to join the forces of the United States, but to unite themselves to the disaffected in Canada, declare the provinces free, and set up another government.

"I am told that regimental officers are already designated for the command of these volunteers.

"That such as above described is the real state of things there can be no doubt.

"It is evidently full of danger, and I am quite surprised at the apparent ignorance or supineness of the government of New York, who represent, evidently, that there is no danger of any violence.

"Our duty is, I think, in the first place, to have officers all along the frontier in whom we have confidence, and to let them understand that there is danger.

"In the next place, it becomes us to take all possible care that no personal violence be used on McLeod. If a mob should kill him, war would be inevitable in ten days. Of this there is no doubt.

"I regret that the attorney-general did not go on and confer with McLeod's counsel, notwithstanding the postponement of the trial. They appear to me to be men of no great force, and who place their main reliance on being able to prove an alibi for their clients. But such a defense does not meet the exigency of the case nor fulfil the duty of this government."

When the trial came on at Utica, in October, 1841, an alibi was established, and McLeod was set free. But the questions of the inviolability of national territory and of apology were yet to be settled.

While the trial of McLeod thus dragged slowly along, the angry feeling toward Great Britain was yet more inflamed by what seemed to be a renewal of her old claim to the right of search. For thirty years and more past she had been engaged in a most honorable endeavor to stop the African slave-trade, and again and again had made treaties with European powers by which British naval officers might search their merchant vessels off the coast of Africa. Portugal and Spain, in 1817; the Netherlands, in 1818; Sweden, in 1824; and France, in 1831 and 1833, had each, by treaty, granted her this privilege, but our own country never would consent. As a consequence, our flag was used by slavers of all nations, and the sight of it off the African coast aroused suspicions as to the character of the ship. For this reason it happened that in 1841 some American merchantmen were seized by British cruisers and held as slavers. In the correspondence which followed, Lord Palmerston claimed a right for British cruisers to visit and search ships carrying our flag in order to ascertain their national character, avowed the intention of his government to exercise this right, and declared that such examination was absolutely necessary; and so the matter stood when Webster became Secretary of State.

Meantime, the interstate slave-trade afforded a new cause of irritation. While the brig *Creole*, loaded with slaves, was on her way from Hampton to New Orleans, the negroes rose, killed one man, shut the crew in the hold, took possession of the vessel, and brought her into the British West Indian port of Nassau. There a few of the slaves were held for murder, and the rest were set free. This incident, following hard upon like action in the cases of the *Comet*, the *Encomium*, and the *Enterprise*, inflamed the South and added new recruits to the party eager for war.

Finally the old question of the northeast boundary, which had been tormenting the people of Maine since 1783, reached a pass where an appeal to force seemed almost at hand.

Dark as the prospect was when Webster went into office, a great change for the better had already taken place. Lord Melbourne's administration had been beaten in the House of Commons, and in August, 1841, he and his colleagues had resigned; Lord Palmerston had been succeeded by Lord Aberdeen as Secretary of Foreign Affairs; Mr. Stevenson, our minister at London, had resigned, and Mr. Everett had been appointed in his stead; and from him, in January, 1842, came the pleasing intelligence that Lord Ashburton would be sent to Washington, as special minister, to settle the boundary and all other questions in dispute between Great Britain and the United States.

Most happily for the peace of the world, the two men now intrusted with the negotiation on which hung the issue of war or peace came to their work in a friendly spirit, and framed the treaty known by their names. In the settlement of the *Caroline* affair, Webster was far too yielding. All that he could wring from Lord Ashburton was an assurance that "no slight or disrespect to the sovereign authority of the United States" was intended by the officers who conducted the raid; an admission "that there was in the hurried execution of this necessary service a violation of territory"; and a statement that, "looking back to what passed at this distance of time, what is, perhaps, most to be regretted is that some explanation and apology for the occurrence was not immediately made." No apology, no expression of regret of any sort, was ever made; and with this acknowledgment that it was *perhaps* to be regretted that no apology was made in 1837, Webster, to his shame, was content. "The President," he wrote his lordship, "is content to receive these acknowledgments, . . . and will make this subject, as a complaint of violation of territory, the topic of no further discussion between the two countries."

To insert in the treaty an article on the subject of impressment was found to be impossible, for Lord Ashburton had no authority to make stipulations. But the occasion was taken to address to the British plenipotentiary a letter which, as Webster truly said, did not "leave the question of impressment where it found it," but "advanced the true doctrine in opposition to it to a higher and stronger foundation"; which declared that "the American government, then, is prepared to say that the practise of impressing American seamen from vessels cannot hereafter be allowed to take place"; and which announced as a principle to be maintained by our government this rule: "In every regularly documented American merchant vessel, the crew who navigate it will find their protection in the flag which is over them."

This declaration, said he, "will stand, because it announces the true principles of public law; because it announces the great doctrine of the equality and independence of nations upon the seas; and because it declares the determination of the government and the people of the United States to uphold those principles and to maintain that doctrine through good report and through evil report, forever. We shall negotiate no more, nor attempt to negotiate more about impressment. We shall not treat hereafter of its limitations to parallels of latitude and longitude. We shall not treat of its allowance or disallowance in broad seas or narrow seas. We shall think no more of stipulating for exemption from its exercise of some of the persons composing the crews. Henceforth the deck of every American vessel is inaccessible for any such purpose. It is protected, guarded, defended by the declaration which I have read, and that declaration will stand."

Out of the *Caroline* affair came the treaty provision for the delivery to justice of persons who, being charged with murder, attempt to murder, piracy, arson, robbery, forgery, or the utterance of forged paper, committed within the territories of the one, shall be found within the territories of the other. With this piece of work Webster was well pleased. "I undertake to say that the article for the extradition of offenders, contained in the treaty of 1842, if there were nothing else in the treaty of any importance, has of itself been of more value to this country, and is of more value to the progress of civilization, the cause of humanity, and the good understanding between nations, than could be readily computed. *. . .* Since the negotiation of this treaty containing this article, we have negotiated treaties with other governments of Europe containing similar provisions, and that between other governments of Europe themselves, treaties have been negotiated containing that provision—a provision never before known to have existed in any of the treaties between European nations.'' He was glad that it had ''proved itself worthy of favor and imitation in the judgment of the most enlightened nations of Europe; and that it has never been complained of by anybody, except by murderers and fugitives and felons themselves.'' Yet it was not wholly new to us, for Jay's treaty, made in 1794, contained a provision for the rendition of persons charged with murder and forgery.

The old and vexed question of the suppression of the African slave trade, so often linked with that of search, was settled by an agreement that each party should keep in service off the coast a squadron of not less than eighty guns, and that the two fleets should act in concert when necessary.

The boundary dispute was put at rest by the determination of a conventional line and the payment to Maine and Massachusetts of large sums of money.

The treaty made and ratified by the Senate, even

the friends of Webster cried out that the time had come for him to leave the cabinet, and were joined by the whole Whig press. After his old-time fashion, he now turned to his friends for advice. Said one: "Your best friends here think there is an insuperable difficulty in your continuing any longer in President Tyler's cabinet." That there might be no doubt where he stood, the State convention of Massachusetts Whigs, when it met in September, read the President out of the party. The duty of the convention was to nominate candidates for State offices: but it went further, and by one resolution announced that the misdeeds of Tyler "left no alternative to the Whigs of Massachusetts but to declare, as they do now declare, their full and final separation from him"; and in another resolution presented Henry Clay to the Whigs of the State as justly entitled to their suffrages "for the first office in the gift of the American people."

On the other hand, strangers, men whose opinion he had not asked, wrote from all parts of the country urging him not to quit the Department of State. Some friends in Boston tendered a dinner, that a chance might be given him to speak in self-defense; but he asked that the dinner be changed to a public reception, and in September, 1842, delivered the "Hard to Coax" speech in Faneuil Hall. He needed just such a defense, and he made it manfully. To the clamor for his resignation he replied: "You know, gentlemen, that twenty years of hon-

ALEXANDER BARING, LORD ASHBURTON.

est and not altogether undistinguished service in
the Whig cause did not save me from an outpouring of wrath which seldom proceeds from Whig
presses and Whig tongues against anybody. I am,
gentlemen, a little hard to coax; but as to being
driven, that is out of the question. I chose to trust
my own judgment, and thinking I was at a post
where I was in the service of my country and could
do it good, I stayed there. . . . No man feels
more highly the advantage of the advice of friends
than I do; but on a question so delicate and important as this I like to choose myself the friends who
are to give me advice; and upon this subject, gentlemen, I shall leave you as enlightened as I found
you.

"I give no pledge; I make no intimation one way
or the other; and I will be as free, when this day
closes, to act, as duty calls, as I was when the dawn
of this day—" The rest of the sentence was lost
in an outburst of applause.

To the State convention of Massachusetts Whigs,
which said that he was not to be their candidate
for the Presidency, he uttered this defiance: "I notice a declaration, made in behalf of all the Whigs
of this commonwealth, of a full and final separation
from the President of the United States. If those
gentlemen saw fit to express their own sentiments
to that extent, there is no objection. Whigs speak
their sentiments everywhere; but whether they may
assume a privilege to speak for others on a point

16

on which those others have not given them authority, is another matter. . . . I am quite ready
to submit to all decisions of Whig conventions on
subjects on which they are authorized to make decisions. But it is quite another question whether
a set of gentlemen, however respectable they may
be as individuals, shall have the power to bind me
on matters which I have not agreed to submit to
their decision at all. . . . And in regard to
the individual who addresses you—what do his
brother Whigs mean to do with him? Where do
they mean to place me? This declaration announces a full and final separation between the
Whigs of Massachusetts and the President. If I
choose to remain in the cabinet, do those gentlemen
mean to say that I cease to be a Whig? I am quite
ready to put that question to the people of Massachusetts.''

As the speech, copied by one newspaper from
another, spread through the country, murmurs of
indignation went up from the Whigs. He was too
great a man, they had been too proud of him, his
services had been too signal, to make it safe to turn
on him and with abuse drive him from the party;
yet they made him feel their high displeasure.
''You see what a dust my speech has raised,'' he
wrote his son Fletcher. ''It is no more than I an-
ticipated. I am sorry the 'Intelligencer' is acting
so foolishly, but that is its own affair. The speech

is printing in pamphlet form in Boston, and will be widely circulated.''

There were other newspapers than the ''Intelligencer'' that commented on his speech. ''If Mr. Webster,'' said one, ''thinks he can dictate to the Whig convention of Massachusetts, he will find that he far overestimates the amount of his influence here.'' ''We will tell him,'' said another, ''what his Whig brethren have done with him: they have nominated Henry Clay for the Presidency, and Massachusetts, as sure as she exists in 1844, will give her electoral vote to that candidate.'' ''Mr. Webster,'' said a third, ''continues to vouch for the Whiggery of Mr. Tyler; but who will vouch for the voucher?'' ''If,'' said another, ''he wishes to share the fate of Mr. Tyler, and go with him to support John C. Calhoun, he is a free agent; if he wishes to give Whig principles and Whig men the benefit of his commanding eloquence, he will be welcomed back to those ranks long honored by his presence and his labors.'' Mr. Berrien of Georgia told a Whig meeting in New York that he had rather be a dog and bay the moon than submit as Webster recommended; and the meeting said ''Amen and amen!'' Some thought the speech indicated that he would leave the cabinet; others that he would stay, as there were many more international difficulties to settle.

Not the least among these was the Oregon boun-

dary, which might have been settled in the treaty
had not the President thought fit to join to it other
issues which could not be hastily discussed. The
plan of Tyler was that Great Britain should persuade Mexico to acknowledge the independence of
Texas and sell us California from latitude 42° to
36° 31'; that she should pay a part of the cost, and
in return take Oregon as far south as the Columbia
River; and that Webster should go to London on a
special mission, with those ends in view. To this the
Senate would not consent. An effort was then made
to persuade Mr. Everett to take the newly created
Chinese mission, and send Webster to London as
Mr. Everett's successor. This too failed, and early
in May the "National Intelligencer" announced
that Daniel Webster had resigned the office of Secretary of State. For months past the newspapers
had been asserting and then denying that he would
surely leave the cabinet; but now, to the joy of the
Locofocos and the Democrats, the report was true.
"There is now nothing to disturb the unanimity
of the cabinet councils," said a Democratic journal, "and the administration may henceforth be
regarded as a unit in sentiment, principles, and purposes." Another spread abroad the report that
the President's son had said, "We have got rid of
Webster at last." That his resignation had been
forced, that the President and his Secretary had
parted bad friends, was long believed, but was not
true. The attacks of the Whig press, the wide-

spread belief that he was no longer a Whig, the effect this belief might have on his chances of securing the Presidential nomination sometime in the future, the determination of Tyler to take up the question of annexing Texas, and the failure to secure the English mission, were the causes which induced him to leave the cabinet.

CHAPTER XIII

WEBSTER was now, for the first time in fifteen years, a private citizen. That he should ever again return to public life seemed far from likely. He had passed his sixtieth birthday, his private affairs were in disorder, and he was free to enjoy the delights of Marshfield, which was to him the dearest spot on earth. But his friends opposed his retirement. Some insisted that he must remove all doubt as to his Whiggery, and sent him as a delegate to the Whig convention at Andover, before which he again spoke in defense of his conduct. Others in New Hampshire asked that they might present his name to the people as a candidate for the Presidency. Still others, in the General Court of Massachusetts, tendered him a reelection to the United States Senate, in place of Mr. Choate, who wished to resign. To this he answered that he would not affect to deny that he much preferred public employment to returning to the bar at his time of life; but his affairs needed attention, he must make a living, and he could ill afford to go back to the Senate and lose the fifteen thousand dollars a year yielded by his practice.

EXTERIOR AND INTERIOR OF
WEBSTER'S LAW OFFICE AT
MARSHFIELD, MASS.

Until March 4, 1845, at least, when Mr. Choate's term would expire, it was, he said, far more important to him to remain in private life than it could be to the nation that he should return to the Senate.

Never was he more mistaken, for an event that he had often contemplated with dread was near at hand. As the campaign opened, the two prospective candidates, Clay and Van Buren, had earnestly striven to put the Texas question out of politics; but Tyler, just before the nominating conventions met, surprised the Senate with a treaty of annexation secretly negotiated with the Texan agent, and made annexation the issue of the day.

Scarcely was this done when the Whig National Convention met at Baltimore and nominated Clay, not by ballot, but with a shout that shook the building. The next day the Whigs held a great ratification meeting, before which Webster appeared to make his peace with the party. Again he solemnly declared himself a Whig, spoke of Clay in the warmest terms, was glad to present the great leader's name to the country as the Whig candidate for the Presidency, and knew of no question before the people on which he did not agree with the candidate. The wild cheers that greeted Webster gave assurance that he was forgiven, and expressed confidence that the reunited and harmonious party was now sure of victory. This confidence was much disturbed when the Democratic convention, a few weeks later, rejected Van Buren, nominated Polk, and demanded the annexation of Texas. Polk was an almost unknown man, and that he should defeat Harry of the West seemed laughable. But the demand for Texas was serious, for now the Whigs must meet that issue or take the consequence of their silence. Webster, in his campaign speech at Valley Forge, spoke plainly and to the point. He was opposed to annexation. But Clay undertook to explain, sent off his Alabama letter, and wrote himself out of the Presidency. The defeat of Clay stunned the Whigs and elated the Democrats, who, carried away by their triumph, passed the joint resolution under which Texas entered the Union as a slave State.

To Webster's plea that it was not important to the country that he should return to public life the Whigs of Massachusetts would now no longer listen, and on March 4, 1845, he once more took his seat in the Senate, as the successor of Rufus Choate, who was a native of Essex, Massachusetts, and a student at Dartmouth College when Webster delivered his great speech in the Dartmouth College case. We are told that Mr. Choate was so powerfully affected by the argument that he determined to study law, a profession in which, in time, he won a reputation as an advocate second to none.

The influence of Webster over Choate, thus early acquired, was never lost; and in their later political careers the two men were closely allied. When Webster left the Senate in 1841, Choate became his successor; when Choate left the Senate in 1845, Webster in turn succeeded him; and in 1852 it was Choate who urged the nomination of Webster for the Presidency before the Whig National Convention at Baltimore.

The annexation of Texas brought war with Mexico; the victories of Taylor and Scott, Kearny and Stockton, brought a chance to secure more territory; fear that the new acquisition might be made slave soil called forth the Wilmot Proviso; and the great struggle for the rights of man was on once more.

During the summer of 1846, President Polk asked Congress for two million dollars "for the purpose of settling all our difficulties with the Mexican Republic." Well knowing that it was intended to use the money to obtain a land cession from Mexico, David Wilmot moved an amendment to the bill, providing that from all territory ceded by Mexico slavery should forever be excluded. The House passed the bill and proviso, but the Senate struck out the proviso, and the House refused to concur. The bill was lost; and when Congress met again a new bill carrying a three-million-dollar appropriation was presented to the House, and the proviso was once more added. This was directly in accord with Webster's anti-expansion views, and a fortnight later he laid upon the table of the Senate two resolutions: the one set forth that war ought not to be waged with Mexico for the purpose

of acquiring new territory out of which to form
new States to be added to the Union; the other that
Mexico ought to be told that the United States did
not want her territory, and would treat for peace
on a liberal basis. A couple of weeks later, when
a resolution much like his was put and voted down,
he spoke out: ''It is due to the best interests of
the country, to its safety, to its peace and harmony,
and to the well-being of the Constitution, to declare at once, to proclaim now, that we want no
new States, nor territory to form new States out of,
as the end of conquest.'' He was not opposed to
a change in the boundary, to such a change as
would give us the port of San Francisco. He was
in favor of the Wilmot Proviso, and voted for it
when the bill with it attached came before the Senate. Indeed, in the autumn, when speaking to a
Whig convention at Springfield, he claimed to have
been its discoverer. ''We hear much, just now,''
he said, ''of a panacea for the dangers and evils
of slavery and slave annexation, which they call
the Wilmot Proviso. . . . I feel some little interest in this matter, sir. Did I not commit myself,
in 1837, to the whole doctrine, fully, entirely? And
I must be permitted to say that I cannot quite consent that more recent discoverers should claim the
merit and take out the patent. I deny the priority
of their invention. Allow me to say, sir, it is not
their thunder.''

The world of politics was now in utter confusion.

Both the great parties were breaking up, and from the fragments that fell off a host of little organizations, "movements" as they were called, were forming. Never before in our annals had so many candidates been nominated by the people. Native Americans, the Liberty party, the Liberty League, the Industrial Congress, Barnburners, Free-soilers, Whigs, and Democrats had each named a candidate of their own or had indorsed one of some other party's choosing.

After the defeat of Clay in 1844, it did seem as if Webster's hour had really come, and that he was the only available leader the Whig party could offer for the Presidency in 1848. Clay, it is true, was never more idolized; but his enemies were many and active, his views on the extension of slavery were opposed to the growing convictions of Northern Whigs, while even his warmest friends had grown very tired of following him always to defeat. A new man was wanted; might not Webster be that man? His belief that slavery was a State institution and could not be meddled with by Congress made him acceptable to Southern Whigs. His services, his abilities, his devotion to the Constitution and the Union, were the admiration of Northern Whigs. His opposition to expansion, to the acquisition of more slave soil, might well bring to his support thousands of old-line Whigs who had been driven by the conduct of Clay into the ranks of the Liberty party. But the prospect, fair as it was, proved a delusion. Webster did not possess one of the attributes of a popular leader. The very greatness of his abilities raised him far above the mass of men, and put him out of touch with them. He inspired awe, but not affection. No mortal man ever thought of coupling his name with any epithet of popular endearment. Jackson was "Old Hickory," "Old Roman"; Harrison was "Old Tip"; Clay was "Harry of the West," "the Mill-boy of the Slashes"; and Taylor "Old Rough-and-Ready": but the senator from Massachusetts was "the Hon. Daniel Webster" to his dying day. Even the cartoonists could find no other name for him than "Black Dan." It was to "Rough-and-Ready," therefore, and not to Daniel Webster, that the Whig masses turned in 1848, when they were done with Henry Clay.

That the hero of Palo Alto and Resaca de la Palma and Monterey and Buena Vista would be nominated by the Whigs was certain as early as the spring of 1847. "The probability now is," Webster wrote to his son in April of that year, "that General Taylor will come in President with a general rush. . . . It is the nature of mankind to carry their favor toward military achievement. No people have ever been found to resist that tendency." This was quite true; yet, when the time came and the convention met, Webster allowed his name to go before it, though certain of defeat. On the first and second ballots he was given twenty-two votes by Maine, New Hampshire, Massachusetts, and New York. On the third ballot he lost one from Maine, three from Massachusetts, and the one from New York. On the fourth and last ballot another vote from Maine and two from New Hampshire left him, and Taylor was triumphantly nominated. The candidate having been named, member after member rose to promise his support to the nominee, and among those who secured recognition from the chair was Mr. Allen, a Conscience Whig of Massachusetts and a warm supporter of Webster. "I think," said he, "I know something of the feelings of my State; I express for myself what I believe to be the sentiments of that State; and I say that we cannot consent that this should go forth as the unanimous vote of this convention, and I will give my reasons." "Amidst cries," says the reporter, "of 'Sit down!' 'Order!' 'Hear him!' 'Go on!' 'Sit down!' 'Let him go on!' we finally caught the words: 'The Whig party of the North are not to be allowed to fill with their statesmen— ['Sit down!' 'Order!' 'Hear him!'] Therefore we declare the Whig party of the Union this day dissolved.' Cheers and hisses now rose in a deafening shout from the excited convention. Member after member jumped to his feet to reply, but they were persuaded by their friends to refrain. 'Let the North answer him!' 'Let Massachusetts answer him!' 'There is better Whiggery there than that!' were the shouts heard from all sides."

When some semblance of order was at last restored, nominations were made for the Vice-Presidency, in the course of which Mr. Ashmun of Massachusetts, rising to withdraw the name of Robert C. Winthrop, denied that Mr. Allen spoke the sense of Massachusetts. In a moment Henry Wilson of the same State was on his feet. "I, for one, will not be bound by the proceedings of this convention," he said. "We have nominated a gentleman, sir, for President of the United States who has stated over and over and over again, to the whole nation, that he did not intend to be bound by the principles or the measures of any party, and that he will not accept the nomination of the Whig party, or the Democratic party, or any party in any portion of the country who will nominate him. Sir, he has said— ['Order, Mr. President, I call the gentleman to order.'] All I asked of this convention was the nomination of a Whig who is unreservedly committed to the principles of the Whig party. But the convention has seen fit to nominate a man who is anything but a Whig; and, sir, I will go home, and, so help me God! I will do all I can to defeat the election of that candidate."

As for the rest of the Massachusetts Whigs, the cotton wing of the party, they accepted the nomination and kept still. Mr. Choate called on them,

RUFUS CHOATE.

"though grieved by the fall of their favorite leader, pierced by a thousand wounds," to rally about Taylor. Mr. Ashmun made a like plea, and shrewdly closed a letter to his constituents with Webster's words to a Whig convention in Faneuil Hall: "In the dark and troubled night that is upon us, I see no star above the horizon promising light to guide us but the intelligent, patriotic, united Whig party of the United States."

Counsel of this sort, however, was not for the great Whig chief, and it was long before he could bring himself to follow the star. He was deeply disappointed. Neither Vermont nor Rhode Island nor Connecticut had cast one vote in his behalf; even Whigs from his own State had deserted him for Taylor: and in the first moments of displeasure he felt sorely tempted to stand aloof. In June he wrote to his son Fletcher, just after the news of Taylor's nomination came: "*Keep entirely quiet till I see you.* I suppose there will be an *émeute,* but it may be quite a question whether you and I and our particular circle of friends had not better stand quite aloof. That is my opinion at present, and until we see into things farther than we can at present. There will probably be enough others to do the work. At any rate, nothing can be gained by sudden action or movement, and therefore by no means commit me or yourself, or our especial and personal friends, till we meet and can consult."

And again, a few days later: "I shall endeavor

to steer my boat with discretion, but it is evident that I must say something, or else it will be said for me by others, and I can see no way but acquiescence in Taylor's nomination—not enthusiastic support, nor zealous approbation, but acquiescence, or forbearance from opposition. This is in accordance with what I said to the Whigs in Boston, viz.: that I should not recommend General Taylor to the people for President, but that if he were fairly nominated by a Whig convention I should not oppose the nomination. I must stand here.''

From this course of conduct his son sought to dissuade him; but he stood firm, and answered: ''I am sorry that I cannot see my way clear to follow your advice entirely. It appears to me necessary that I should express publicly either acquiescence or dissatisfaction with the nomination. I have certainly said often that I should not recommend General Taylor; but I have said, too, always, at the same time, that I should not oppose his election if nominated. Beyond that I propose to say nothing, except in favor of the general Whig cause.

''These Northern proceedings can come to nothing useful to you or to me. The men are all low in their objects. The Abolitionists will adhere to Mr. Hale. The Barnburners will nominate Mr. Niles. If the [illegible] men at Worcester were to ask to put me on their ticket, what would it all come to? I could not consent to that, with so little show of strength as they now put forth. On the other hand, suppose I acquiesce in General Taylor's nomination. He will or will not be chosen; if chosen (as I incline to think he will be), it may be for your interests not to have opposed him; as to mine, it is quite indifferent. I have, for myself, no object whatever.

"If he is not chosen, things can stand no worse. Then, on the general ground, it seems to me I must not in consistency abandon the support of Whig principles. My own reputation will not allow of this. I cannot be silent without being reproached when such a case is being pressed upon the country.

"I agree it is a difficult and doubtful question; but I think the safest way is to overlook the nomination, as not being the main thing, and to continue to maintain the Whig cause.

"We shall see, but I think we shall come out right."

By September this uncertainty has passed away. His course is clear before him, and Fletcher is assured: "I see no way but to fall in and acquiesce. The run is all that way. We can do no good by holding out. We shall only isolate ourselves. Northern opposition is too small and narrow to rely on.

"I must say *something, somewhere,* soon. My purpose is to enlarge the necessity of a change of administration, to say something of the North and its expectations, and, on the whole, to express a

17

hope for Taylor. I must either do this, or go right into opposition.''

Webster had now reached another and the final turning-point in his public career. Had he been wise, he would have taken the turn which led him ''right into opposition.'' Judged in the light of every speech he had made since the Missouri Compromise, he was a Free-soiler, and his place was with that party. So far as principles were concerned, the platform of that party might have been made up of extracts from his own public utterances. For a man so minded the Whigs were not fit companions. But Webster remained a Whig, and, as he was obliged to speak out, accepted an invitation to address his friends at Marshfield in September. ''My purpose in this speech,'' he wrote a friend, ''was exactly this: first, to make out a clear case for all true Whigs to vote for him [Taylor]; second, to place myself in a condition of entire independence, fearing nothing, and hoping nothing personally, from his failure or success; thirdly, and most especially, to show the preposterous conduct of those Whigs who make a secession from their party and take service under Van Buren.'' Just why a Whig who believed in the exclusion of slavery from the Territories, who was opposed to the formation of more slave States, should vote for Taylor, a slaveholder, rather than Van Buren, a Free-soiler, he failed to make clear. But when he told his neighbors that the nomination of Tay-

lor "stands by itself, without a precedent or justi-
fication from anything in our previous history";
that it was a nomination "not fit to be made"; that
the "sagacious, wise, far-seeing doctrine of avail-
ability lay at the root of the whole matter," he succeeded, so far as Taylor was concerned, in placing
himself "in a condition of entire independence."
This he well knew, and feeling that he could have
little influence at Washington, another fit of political blues seized him, and he wrote: "The general
result of my reflections up to the present moment
is that it will be most expedient for me to leave
Congress at the end of the session and attend to
my own affairs." From the Slough of Despond
his friends raised him by insisting, after the great
Whig triumph, that he should take his old place at
the head of the Department of State. "A friend
has just said to me, 'The great question in State
Street is, Can Mr. Webster be prevailed upon to
be Secretary of State?' My dear friend, I am old
and poor and proud. All these things beckon me
to retirement, to take care of myself—and, as I cannot act the first post, to act none." Yet he would
not commit himself to a refusal of the place should
it be offered, and went to Washington in December, 1848, in a better state of mind. During the
next three months his letters show a lingering hope
that the office may be tendered, a well-founded
doubt that it would be, and an earnest desire to be
left "to my profession, my studies, or my ease."

To some extent this wish was granted. The invitation to join the cabinet never came. Once more a kind Fate preserved him for greater things. Had he entered the cabinet of Taylor, he would have been a silent spectator of the struggle for the Compromise of 1850, and the most famous of all his speeches would never have been made.

CHAPTER XIV

THE SEVENTH OF MARCH

WHILE Webster thus waited and wondered what Taylor would do, the South and the North were in bitter strife over the territory wrung from Mexico—the one to open it to slavery, the other to keep it, as Mexico had made it four-and-twenty years before, free. How to turn free soil into slave soil was a hard question to settle, and many plans were presented and rejected before a senator proposed to spread the Constitution over the new Territory by act of Congress. This done, all trouble would be over: for, under the Constitution, slaves were property; could, as such, be taken into the Territory by immigrants; and, once in, must be protected. With slaves in the Territory, the institution of slavery would quickly follow, and all trace of freedom be swept from the soil. But just here a new difficulty arose: Could the Constitution be spread over the Territories? Calhoun declared it could be so extended; Webster maintained that it could not: and the two fell into a debate of no little interest to us at this moment. The question was the status, under the Constitution, of newly acquired soil. In the opinion of

Webster, such territory was the property of, not part of, the United States. The Constitution was confined to the United States, to the States united under it; was extended over nothing else, and could extend over nothing, "because a Territory while a Territory does not become a part, and is no part, of the United States." "The Constitution," said Calhoun, "interprets itself. It pronounces itself to be the supreme law of the land." "What land?" said Webster. "The land," was Calhoun's reply. "The Territories of the United States are a part of the land. It is the supreme law, not within the limits of the States of this Union merely, but wherever our flag waves, wherever our authority goes, the Constitution in part goes; not all its provisions certainly, but all its suitable provisions."

"The 'land,' I take it," said Webster, "means the land over which the Constitution is established, or, in other words, it means the States united under the Constitution. The Constitution no more says that the Constitution shall be the supreme law of the land than it says that the laws of Congress shall be the supreme law of the land. It declares that the Constitution and the laws of Congress passed under it shall be the supreme law of the land. . . . According to the gentleman's reasoning, the Constitution extends over the Territories as supreme law, and no legislation on the subject is necessary. This would be tantamount to saying that the moment territory is attached to the United States, all the laws of the United States, as well as the Constitution of the United States, become the governing rule of men's conduct and of the rights of property, because they are declared to be the law of the land, the laws of Congress being the supreme law of the land as well as the Constitution of the United States. The precise question is, Whether a Territory, while it remains on a territorial state, is a part of the United States? I maintain that it is not."

In the end these views prevailed. The attempt to extend the Constitution failed; no government was provided for California or New Mexico, and the question went over to the next Congress. At this the South, firmly united on the question of slavery in the new Territories, grew alarmed and angry. The old spirit of disunion again arose, threats of secession were heard once more, and a call went out for a State-Rights convention, to meet at Nashville beside the bones of Andrew Jackson. All the old grievances that the South had against the North were revived and asserted. The failure duly to execute the fugitive-slave law, the "underground railroad," the activity of the demand for the abolition of slavery and the slave-trade in the District of Columbia, were now declared unendurable. To make matters worse, a quarrel broke out between Texas and the federal government over the boundary of New Mexico, and the people of

California, taking matters into their own hands, made a free-State constitution, established a State government, and asked admission into the Union as a free State.

With all these burning questions under hot debate, it may well be believed that the country awaited the meeting of Congress with feelings of no common sort. On that body most assuredly rested the momentous question of peace or war. By it was to be decided whether the house divided against itself should stand or fall; whether there should be within the limits of what was then the United States one people, one government, one flag, or two republics—one of States where black men were slaves, the other of States where the negro was free. Nor was the Congress then assembled less interesting than its work. Never had there been gathered in the two chambers so many men whose names later events have made familiar to us. In the Senate were now brought together, for the last time, Webster, Calhoun, and Clay, leaders of the old parties, and Jefferson Davis and Stephen A. Douglas, soon to head the wings of a hopelessly divided democracy. There, too, were Salmon P. Chase and William H. Seward, destined to become chiefs of a party yet unformed; Hannibal Hamlin, the first Vice-President under Lincoln; Samuel Houston, who led the Texans on the field of San Jacinto, and twice served as president of that republic; and Thomas Hart Benton, now about to close a term of almost thirty years of continuous service in the Senate.

To this distinguished body Clay returned fully determined to take little part in its proceedings. He would support Whig measures, but would neither aid nor oppose the administration. He would be a calm looker-on, rarely speaking, and even then merely for the purpose of pouring oil on the troubled waters. But he had not been many days in Washington before he was convinced that the talk of disunion was serious, that the Union was really in danger, that old associates were turning to him, and that he must again take his place as leader. During three weeks the House of Representatives wrangled and disputed over the choice of a Speaker, and this time was used by Clay to prepare a plan to serve as the basis of a compromise. By the middle of January, 1850, his work was ready, and one cold evening he called on Webster, and went over the scheme, and asked for aid. This was conditionally promised, and a week later Clay unfolded his plan in a set of resolutions, and at the end of another week explained his purpose in a great speech delivered before a deeply interested audience. A rumor that he would speak on a certain day brought men and women from cities as far away as New York to swell the crowd that filled the Senate chamber, choked every entrance, and stood in dense masses in the halls and passages. Fatigue and anxiety were telling on him. He could with difficulty climb the long flight of steps and make his way to his place on the floor. But the eager faces of the throng, the seriousness of the plea he was about to make, and the shouts of applause that rose from floor and gallery when he stood up to speak, and were taken up with yet greater vigor by the crowd without, gave him new strength. So wild was the cheering of those beyond the chamber doors, and so long did it continue, that he could not be heard in the room, and the president was forced to order the hallways to be cleared. Again Clay spoke during two days, and on the second showed such signs of physical distress that senators repeatedly interrupted him with offers to adjourn. But he would not yield, and went on till he had finished.

Clay having spoken, it was certain that Calhoun would follow, and letter after letter now came to Webster imploring him to raise his voice for the preservation of the Union, and speak as he had never done before.

"Pardon this intrusion and the boldness implied in this address," wrote an earnest antislavery leader. "I deprecate the appearance of presuming to give counsel to you, whom I regard with sincere admiration. But I must bear the folly of this presumption, for I cannot but obey the impulse that I have long felt to express to you, sir, my deep conviction that if Daniel Webster would only throw that great nature which heaven has given him into

the great cause of the world, the cause of human
freedom, his fellow-citizens, his fellow-men, would
behold such a demonstration of personal power as
is seldom given to the world to witness. . . .
You once said of a professional friend, that 'when
his case was stated, it was argued.' Of no man
can this be said with more entire truth than of you.
If, taking liberty for your light, you cast your
broad glance over the history and state of the country—if, seeing, as many think you could not fail
to see, how slavery has *interfered*, and is *interfering*, not with the property, but with the rights,
with the inmost hearts of freemen, making them
its tools and supporters, you were then to tell the
country, in that grand and simple way in which
no man resembles you, what you see, *stating the
great case* so that it would be argued once for all
and forever, you would not only render the whole
country, North *and* South, the greatest possible
service, but you would be conscious of a compensation in your own being which even your great
power could not begin to compute."

As time passed and Webster made no sign of an
intent to speak, the appeals grew more urgent.

"Do it, Mr. Webster," said an unknown admirer,
"as you can do it, like a bold and gifted statesman
and patriot; reconcile the North and South, and
preserve the Union. Blessings will attend you if
you succeed, and your name will be embalmed in
the hearts of your countrymen.

"You will be greater than he whom we call the Father of his Country. He achieved its independency through the valor of our countrymen and the aid of France. I venerate Washington! But now the aspect is changed. He secured the liberty of the colonies. *Whoever preserves the Union secures the liberty of the world.*

"Allow me in times like these to address you in a familiar style. Offer, Mr. Webster, a liberal compromise to the South, and, my word for it, the North will sustain you.

"Pardon the freedom I use in addressing you. I am an humble practitioner of medicine—a democrat—but I go for the 'Constitution as it is, and the Union as it is.' "

"Sir," wrote another, "if you make a speech on the Compromise Bill that will settle the controversy between the North and South, please send me one of those speeches."

"I pray you," said a third, "to pardon my intruding on you for a moment at a time when your whole mind is so much engrossed by the important events which call for all your thoughts and powers. Let me, however, tell you in a few words that the hope of this community never before so hung on the wisdom, eloquence, and power of one man as it does at this moment on yours. Your speech on 'Foot's resolution' was a turning-point in your own life. Your speech this week may be the turning-point in the life of this nation. God

knows I mean no empty flattery when I say that
I believe you, and you only, adequate to 'set right'
the mind of the whole country, North and South,
on the great question which so agitates it. The
same intellect, the same wisdom, the same power
of demonstration and force of thought and language which *turned back* the Niagara torrent of
public sentiment and opinion in the former case
can now show to the South itself where right and
reason lie. The 'equilibrium' plan, by which slavery is to repress and keep back the institutions of
freedom, is a confession of the weakness of slavery.
It shows what must be its own destiny in case of
disunion and if left to itself. Why is it that the
slave States need new guards? Simply because
free institutions are outstripping them. In this
age, can it be dreamed of that freedom shall be
kept back because slavery cannot go forward? I
cannot now name one mortal man in the whole
circle of my acquaintance who would now, or who
ever heretofore would, meddle with slavery in the
slave States. Why should the slave States meddle
with my rights by insisting on an extension of the
inequality of representation by which one man own-
ing five slaves has as much power as *three* Northern farmers, lawyers, mechanics, or merchants?
This is the point which galls me. I am sadly defi-
cient in philanthropy, and don't know that I should
object to own slaves if I lived in a slave State, but
it is this political preponderance which gives to

one man's property so much power over me that
I had rather fight than submit to any further increase of it. How would it do to suggest the idea
that if they wish to carry slaves with them into
new States and Territories, such slaves shall not
form a basis of representation?

"I was struck this morning with a remark of
young Mr. Rives, that no man's position in the
land was equal to yours for so displaying and
putting the whole case as to satisfy even the reasonable and reasoning portion of the Northern people as to what is the enlarged and right view of
the whole question—because your position has always been strictly national, while Mr. Calhoun's
has been strictly *sectional*. He added that he looked
for the greatest argument now that this country
had ever produced. I need not repeat to you the
ardent expressions which he used as to your ability to give it."

Appeals of this sort were quite unnecessary, for
Webster was cautiously and deliberately deciding
what was the wisest course to take. In a letter
written as late as the middle of February he said:
"There will be no disunion, no disruption. Things
will cool off. California will come in. New Mexico will be postponed. No bones will be broken,
and in a month all this will be more apparent."
In another letter, written at the same time, he
declares: "I do not partake in any degree in those
apprehensions which you say some of our friends

entertain of the dissolution of the Union or the breaking up of the government. There is no danger, be assured, and so assure our friends. I have, thus far, upon a good deal of reflection, thought it advisable for me to hold my peace. If a moment should come when it will be advisable that any temperate, *national*, and practical speech which I can make would be useful, I shall do the best I can. Let the North keep cool.'' Another week's reflection convinced him that a national speech must be made, and on the 22d of February he wrote the same friend: ''As time goes on I will keep you advised by telegraph, as well as I can, on what day I shall speak. As to what I shall say you can guess nearly as well as I can. I mean to make a Union speech, and discharge a clear conscience.'' His biographer assures us that ''there was but little written preparation for it,'' and that ''all that remains of such preparation is on two small scraps of paper.'' Yet there are among his papers seventeen sheets of notes, many of which are written on both sides of the paper.

On the 4th of March, while Webster was still at work on his speech, Calhoun, then fast sinking into his grave, attended the Senate. He was far too feeble to bear the fatigue of speaking, so his argument was read, in the midst of profound silence, by Senator Mason of Virginia. The second of the great triumvirate having now been heard, it soon became noised abroad that Webster would reply on March 7; and on that day, accordingly, the floors, galleries, and antechambers of the Senate were so densely packed that it was with difficulty that the members reached their seats. Mr. Walker of Wisconsin had the floor to finish a speech begun the day before; but when he had risen and looked about him, he said: "Mr. President, this vast audience has not come together to hear me, and there is but one man, in my opinion, who can assemble such an audience. They expect to hear him, and I feel it my duty, therefore, as it is my pleasure, to give the floor to the senator from Massachusetts."

Webster then rose, and after thanking the senator from Wisconsin and Mr. Seward, the senator from New York, for their courtesy in yielding the floor, began that speech which he named "The Constitution and the Union," but which his countrymen have ever since called by the day of the month on which it was delivered.

The scene now presented in the Senate is thus described by one of the newspaper letter-writers of the day: "After a long experience, and having enjoyed the good fortune to be present on many of those occasions which form epochs in public affairs, I have never before witnessed one on which there was deeper feeling enlisted or more universal anxiety to catch the most distant echo of the speaker's voice. Had the accommodations been tenfold, they would have failed to satisfy the demand made by every age and sex and condition. The spectacle from the thronged galleries was one of imposing interest and novelty. No spot was left untenanted. All seemed to wait with anxiety when the great orator would appear upon the scene.

"Mr. Webster rose in the full majesty of his commanding person, grave and dignified, and seeming to realize the greatness of the occasion which enlisted his services and the large expectation which was excited.

"It is conceded on all hands that Mr. Webster has made an important movement, one which will exercise large influence with the country and affect the settlement of the question in issue seriously. This event has occasioned much sensation, and, if the signs are to be trusted, a favorable reaction. Mr. Webster has assumed a great responsibility, and, whether he succeeds or fails, the courage with which he has come forward at least entitles him to the respect of the country."

The speech did indeed make a great sensation, and for a while every mail brought bundles of letters of praise and requests for copies of it. Said one: "I was highly gratified in reading your admirable patriotic and powerful speech in relation to the new Territories. It was a bold, independent, and dignified discharge of the high duties devolved upon you. The *crisis* required that the ablest men should come forth, in the majesty of their strength, and rebuke the fanatics and demagogues through-

18

out the land who, by their mad and treasonable efforts, have basely attempted to shatter the massive pillars of the Union.

"The obstructionists, the impracticable, the unprincipled, and the ignorant will evince their wrath at the signal defeat which they must perceive awaits them; but you are protected against their vindictive assaults by the holy buckler of patriotism, and all honest men *now* and for all coming time will be grateful for such a fearless and noble illustration of devotion to the stability, prosperity, and glory of the Republic."

Said another: "I have read carefully and with reflection your speech of Thursday last. It appears to me if Washington had arisen from his tomb and addressed the Senate on that day, he would have uttered the words of your speech.

"It bears throughout the impress of one lifted up above the mists of passion, prejudice, and faction, surveying with a clear vision all that is passing below, and truthfully stating it. Divested of sectional feeling, forgetful of the character of a special representative, the words of truth and solemnness fell from the lips of one impelled by a sense of the general good."

Addresses of approbation came to him from citizens of Boston, of Newburyport, and of Medford, from the inhabitants of towns on the Kennebec River in Maine, and from innumerable places all over the South, the West, and the Middle States, coupled with calls for printed copies of the speech.

"The clamor for speeches South and West is incredible," he wrote his son. "Two hundred thousand will not supply the demand." To a friend he wrote: "Letters come in thickly and all one way. As soon as we can get a decent edition out, I mean to send a copy to the members of the Massachusetts legislature, and every judge, lawyer, justice of the peace, doctor, and clergyman in the commonwealth. And I would send thousands more, under my own frank, if I could afford it. But other people will send many also."

"I have received yours," he informs his son, "and will send one thousand speeches by express to-morrow."

By the end of March "one hundred and twenty thousands have gone off," and, as the demand showed no decline, "I suppose that by the first day of May two hundred thousand will have been distributed from Washington."

No speech ever delivered in the Senate of the United States produced such an effect on the country. Compromisers, conservative men, business men with Southern connections, those willing to see the Union saved by any means, rallied to his support, and loaded him with unstinted praise. But the antislavery men, the abolitionists, the Free-soilers, and many Northern Whigs attacked him bitterly.

"Webster," said Horace Mann, "is a fallen star! Lucifer descending from heaven!" "By this speech," said Giddings, "a blow was struck at freedom and the constitutional rights of the free States which no Southern arm could have given." Theodore Parker was sure that "not a hundred prominent men in all New England acceded to the speech," and for the moment the estimate seemed to be correct. "Webster," said Sumner, "has placed himself in the dark list of apostates." In the opinion of hosts of his fellow-countrymen, he was indeed an apostate. He had changed his creed; he had broken from his past; he had deserted the cause of human liberty; he had fallen from grace. When Whittier named him Ichabod, and mourned for him in verse as one dead, he did but express the feeling of half New England:

> Let not the land once proud of him
>   Insult him now,
> Nor brand with deeper shame his dim,
>   Dishonored brow.
>
> But let its humbled sons, instead,
>   From sea to lake,
> A long lament, as for the dead,
>   In sadness make.
>
>   .   .   .   .   .   .
>
> Then, pay the reverence of old days
>   To his dead fame;
> Walk backward, with averted gaze,
>   And hide the shame!

When news of the speech reached Boston, the House of Representatives were debating resolu-

tions declaring that Massachusetts could accept no compromise which called on her to abandon principles she had so firmly held and so often repeated, and here too Webster was condemned in vigorous language. He is, said one member, "a recreant son of Massachusetts who misrepresents her in the Senate." "Daniel Webster," said Henry Wilson, "will be a fortunate man if God, in his sparing mercy, shall preserve his life long enough for him to repent of this act and efface this stain on his name." At a great meeting held in Faneuil Hall to condemn the conduct of Webster, the Seventh-of-March speech was described as "alike unworthy of a wise statesman and a good man." Said Theodore Parker: "I know of no deed in American history done by a son of New England to which I can compare this, but the act of Benedict Arnold." Whig journals in New England, Whig journals all over the North, a large part of the religious press, even the Boston "Atlas," edited by an old and true friend of Webster, now turned against him.

The attack by the press, the expressions of horror that rose from New England, Webster felt keenly; but the absolute isolation in which he was left by his New England colleagues cut him to the quick, and in his letters he complains of this bitterly: "Thus far I have not one concurring vote from Massachusetts. I regret this much, but I hope I may be able to stand, though I stand alone. At any rate, I shall stand till I fall. I will not sit down."

"I cannot well describe to you, my dear sir," he wrote in December, "what my feelings were for five months, during which no one of my colleagues manifested the slightest concurrence in my sentiments, and at the same time I knew that sincere men and good Whigs at home disapproved or doubted. It was natural enough that the speech of March 7th should produce a spark."

That he should now make a public defense of his position was quite proper, and this he did in a series of letters in response to addresses from citizens of New England. To eight hundred well-known men of Boston, who thanked him for his "broad, national, and patriotic views," he said: "In my judgment, there is no sufficient cause for the continuance of the existing alienation between the North and the South. . . . So far as the question of slavery or no slavery applies to the newly acquired Territories, there is, in my judgment, no real and practical point of importance in dispute. There is not, and there cannot be, slavery, as I firmly believe, either in California, New Mexico, or Utah. And if this be so, why continue the controversy on a mere abstraction?"

In his reply to the citizens of Newburyport, he reviewed at great length the history of the passage and effect of the fugitive-slave law of 1793; complained that the greatest clamor and outcry "against the cruelty and enormity of the reclamation of slaves" came from "quarters where no

such reclamation has ever been made, or, if ever
made, where the instances are so exceedingly few
and far between as to have escaped general knowledge''; and asked, what is there, then, ''to justify
the passionate appeals, the vehement and empty
declamations, the wild and fanatical conduct of
both men and women, which have so long disturbed and so much disgraced the commonwealth
and the country''? When answering the citizens
of the Kennebec River towns he made long extracts from the writings of travelers to prove that
his description of New Mexico was correct, that
''this whole country is of very little value,'' and
that it is ''just about as probable that African slavery will be introduced into New Mexico, and there
established, as it is that it will be established on
Mars Hill, or the side of the White Mountains.''

The purpose of Webster was not to put slavery
in nor shut it out of the new Territories, nor make
every man in the North a slave-catcher, nor bid
for Southern support in the coming election. He
sought a final and lasting settlement of a question
which threatened the permanence of the Union
and the Constitution, and Clay's ''comprehensive
scheme of adjustment,'' he believed, would effect
this settlement. The abolition, the antislavery, the
Free-soil parties, were to him but ''Northern movements'' that would ''come to nothing.'' The great
debate of 1850 he regarded as idle talk that interrupted consideration of the tariff. Never, in his

opinion, had history made record of a case of such mischief arising from angry debates and disputes, both in the government and the country, on questions of so very little real importance. Therein lay his fatal mistake. The great statesman had fallen behind the times, and it was perhaps well for him that he was now removed from the Senate to the Department of State.

The Seventh-of-March speech had been followed on the eleventh by the famous "higher law" speech of Seward, by the appointment of a committee of thirteen to consider the resolutions of Clay and others, and by a report from the committee early in May. Seven things were proposed: that the admission of a State or States formed out of Texas should be postponed; that California should be admitted as a State; that all the rest of the country acquired from Mexico should be made into two Territories, to be called New Mexico and Utah, and organized without the Wilmot Proviso; that the admission of California and the organization of New Mexico and Utah should be provided for in one bill; that into this bill should go a provision to pay Texas for ceding a part of the great territory she claimed; that there should be a new fugitive-slave law; and, finally, that the slave-trade should be prohibited in the District of Columbia.

To this scheme of adjustment Taylor was strongly opposed; but while it was still under debate, and far from acceptance, he died, on the 9th of July, 1850. Millard Fillmore then became President of the United States, and on the 22d of July Webster entered the new cabinet as Secretary of State. He was now an observer, but by no means a passive observer, of the passage of the compromise measures by Congress.

Change of place, however, brought no change of views, and his hatred of the Free-soilers and abolitionists grew stronger and stronger. To him these men were a band of sectionalists, narrow of mind, wanting in patriotism, without a spark of national feeling, and quite ready to see the Union go to pieces if their own selfish ends were gained. Free-soilers and abolitionists were all one to him, and as such were attacked in language unworthy of the great man. In June, 1850, he declared to a friend:

"I believe, my dear sir, that the political men of lead and consequence of both the great parties are sound on great constitutional questions. They are *national*, and justly appreciate great national objects. But there are thousands in each party who are more concerned for State than for national politics, whose objects are all small and their views all narrow; and then, again, this abolition feeling has quite turned the heads of thousands. Depend upon it,—indeed, I dare say you think so as well as I,—there are many men at the North who do not speak out what they wish, but who really desire to break up the Union. And some of these are men of influence and standing, and are or have been in public life.

"Things begin to look better. There is evidently a reaction in the South; some impression has been made in New York. Most of the New England States are now pretty right on the Union questions; and Massachusetts, who has so strangely bolted from her sphere, may, I hope, be brought back to it. On the whole, I believe the worst is past."

In September he assures another friend that he "had much rather see a respectable Democrat elected to Congress than a professed Whig tainted with any degree of Free-soil doctrines or abolitionism. Men who act upon some principle, though it be a wrong principle, have usually some consistency of conduct; and they are therefore less dangerous than those who are looking for nothing but increased power and influence, and who act simply on what seems expedient for their purposes at the moment."

In October he writes to the President: "The politics of Massachusetts are in a state of utter confusion. Many Whigs *are afraid* to act a manly part, lest they should lose the State government. They act a most mean part in their courtship of abolitionism. . . . Seven imported Unitarian priests are now candidates for public office,—viz.: members of Congress,—besides a host of others who offer for the legislature. These are all Free-soil or abolition men. The postmaster at Lowell is

represented to be a brawling abolitionist, preaching
daily the duty of resistance to the fugitive-slave
law. I shall inquire into this when I return to
Boston.'' In another letter Syracuse is called
''that laboratory of abolitionism, libel, and trea-
son.'' In a speech at Capon Springs, Virginia
(now West Virginia), after ridiculing Seward's
''higher law,'' he said: ''It is the code, however,
of the fanatical and factious abolitionists of the
North.'' But ''the secessionists of the South'' were
''learned and eloquent, . . . animated and
full of spirit, . . . high-minded and chival-
rous. . . . I am not disposed to reproach these
gentlemen or speak of them with disrespect.'' The
Constitution, despite his reply to Hayne and his
answer to Calhoun, was now found to contain at
least one ''compact.'' ''How absurd it is to suppose,'' said he to the Capon Springs audience,
''that, when different parties enter into a compact
for certain purposes, either can disregard any one
provision, and expect, nevertheless, the other to
observe the rest! . . . I have not hesitated to
say, and I repeat, that if the Northern States refuse, wilfully and deliberately, to carry into effect
that part of the Constitution which respects the
restoration of fugitive slaves, and Congress provide no remedy, the South would no longer be
bound to observe the compact.''

In the opinion of the Free-soil and antislavery
people, the fugitive-slave law was the most hate-

ful of all the compromise measures. In the opinion of Webster, it was not only wise, but absolutely necessary. Indeed, during the early months of 1850 he framed a bill of his own, had it in his desk ready for introduction when he stood up to make the Seventh-of-March speech, and did introduce it in June. In detail it was quite unlike the bill reported by the committee. No provision was made for the gathering of a posse to prevent a rescue, nor for the use of the army and navy, nor for the punishment of a marshal from whom a fugitive escaped. The negro claimed as a slave was to be heard in his own defense, and if, after the nature of an oath had been made plain to him, he swore he was not the claimant's property, he was to be tried before a jury, each man of which was to be paid fifty cents for his pains. This marked difference, however, did not in the least affect Webster's eagerness to uphold the bill reported by committee when once it became a law. Again and again, in his answers to calls to speak at Union meetings, he bitterly denounces those who threaten to oppose its execution, and to the very last gave his hearty approval to the compromise measures. "I trust," he wrote in April, 1852, to one of his countless admirers, "there is not a man in the country who doubts my approbation of those measures which are usually called 'compromise measures,' or my fixed determination to uphold them steadily and firmly. Nothing but a deep sense of duty led me to take the part which I did take in bringing about their adoption by Congress, and that same sense of duty remains with unabated force. I am of opinion that those measures, one and all, were necessary and expedient, and ought to be adhered to by all friends of the Constitution and all lovers of their country. That one among them which appears to have given the greatest dissatisfaction— I mean the fugitive-slave law—I hold to be a law entirely constitutional, highly proper, and absolutely essential to the peace of the country. Such a law is demanded by the plain written words of the Constitution, and how any man can wish to abrogate or destroy it, and at the same time say that he is a supporter of the Constitution, and willing to adhere to those provisions in it which are clear and positive injunctions and restraints, passes my power of comprehension. My belief is that when the passions of men subside, and reason and true patriotism are allowed to have their proper sway, the public mind, North and South, will come to a proper state upon these questions. I do not believe that further agitation can make any considerable progress at the North. The great mass of the people, I am sure, are sound, and have no wish to interfere with such things as are by the Constitution placed under the exclusive control of the separate States. I have noticed, indeed, not without regret, certain proceedings to which you have alluded; and in regard to these I have to say that gentlemen may not think it necessary or proper that they should be called upon to affirm, by resolution, that which is already the existing law of the land. That any positive movement to repeal or alter any or all the compromise measures would meet with any general encouragement or support I do not at all believe. But, however, that may be, my own sentiments remain, and are likely to remain, quite unchanged. I am in favor of upholding the Constitution in the general and all its particulars. I am in favor of respecting its authority and obeying its injunctions, and to the end of my life shall do all in my power to fulfil honestly and faithfully all its provisions. I look upon the compromise measures as a just, proper, fair, and final adjustment of the questions to which they relate, and no re-agitation of those questions, no new opening of them, no effort to create dissatisfaction with them, will ever receive from me the least countenance or support, concurrence or approval, at any time or under any circumstances.''

The Seventh-of-March speech, the elaborate and repeated defenses of the compromise measures, the avowed sympathy with Southern views, the earnest support of the fugitive-slave law, now led the Eastern Whigs to see in Webster an available candidate for the Presidency. The failing health of Clay and his many defeats put his nomination out of the question. But to the voting masses the name of Webster made no appeal. They were steadily turning toward another military chieftain. They had nominated the hero of Tippecanoe, and had won; they had nominated the hero of Buena Vista, and had won. Why not nominate the hero of Cerro Gordo, of Churubusco, of Chapultepec, and win again? As between "Old Fuss-and-Feathers" and the "Defender of the Constitution," the people found it easy to choose. Nevertheless, the friends of Webster thought best to make the attempt to effect a union of Whig sentiment in his favor, and two appeals were soon before the public. One was the work of Mr. Everett, the other came from the pen of William M. Evarts, and both fell flat. Even his friends saw this, and when the Whig convention was about to meet at Baltimore, Mr. Choate, who was to present the name of Webster, went to Washington to warn him of the hopelessness of the attempt. But he found the great man so sure of victory that he had not the heart to tell him, and went on to Baltimore. There, on the first ballot, the vote stood: Fillmore, 133; Scott, 131; Webster, 29; necessary to a choice, 147. That he was beaten was plain; but it was clear that his friends might say whether Scott or Fillmore should be the candidate. They chose to fight to the end, and fifty-three ballots were taken before Scott received 159 and was declared the nominee.

In public Webster bore his defeat like a man; but his letters show how keenly he felt the disappointment. To his son he wrote:

"I confess I grow inclined to cross the seas. I meet here so many causes of vexation and humiliation, growing out of the events connected with the convention, that I am pretty much decided and determined to leave the department early in August, and either go abroad or go into obscurity."

But the sting of defeat was sharpest when calls without number came to him to give aid to the party candidate. Most of them he would not answer; but to one he replied:

MARSHFIELD, October 12, 1852.

GENTLEMEN: I received only yesterday your communication of the 24th of September; and, among a great number of similar letters, it is the only one I answer. . . . If I were to do what you suggest, it would gratify not only you and your friends, but that great body of implacable enemies who have prevented me from being elected President of the United States. You all know this, and now how can I be called upon to perform any act of humiliation for their gratification, or the promotion of their purposes?

But, gentlemen, I do not act from personal feeling. It is with me a matter of principle and character, and I have now to state to you that no earthly consideration could induce me to say anything or do anything from which it might be inferred, directly or indirectly, that I concur in the Baltimore nomination, or that I should give it, in any way, the sanction of my approbation. If I were to do such act, I should feel my cheeks already scorched with shame by the reproaches of posterity.

It was long the popular belief that disappointed ambition, chagrin over the loss of the Presidential nomination, was the cause of Webster's death; but that such was the case may well be doubted. He was now an old man, far on in his seventy-first year. His health had long been failing; his strong efforts in behalf of the compromise measures had impaired it still further; and his end was inevitably near. That his great disappointment hastened the end is quite likely, for from the June day when the Baltimore convention adjourned he broke rapidly, and in the early morning of October 24, 1852, he died at Marshfield. Clay had preceded him by four months.

INDEX

INDEX

Aberdeen, Lord, succeeds Palmerston, 272

Abolition, 247; right of petition for, 250

Abolitionists, 241, 242; petitions of, 245, 246

Adams, John, oration on, 142–145

Adams, John Q., Webster on election of, 123–124, 125; the "coalition," 126–129; elected President, 130; the White House, 137

"Address to the People of South Carolina," 194–195

Allegheny County, sends Webster delegates, 235

Alton, visited by Webster, 239

Andover, Mass., Webster speaks at, 284

Annexation of Louisiana, 243; of Florida, 244; of Texas, 244

"Anthology, The Monthly," 47

Anti-Masons, question Webster, 235

Antislavery, 241, 242, 243; growth of, 249; Webster's attitude toward, in 1839, 250

Antislavery Society, the American, 241

"Appeal to the Old Whigs," — pamphlet written by Webster, 44

Ashburton, Lord, on the *Caroline* affair, 272; given no authority on subject of impressment, 273

Bangor, Webster speaks at, 231

Bank of the United States, Jackson's veto of the bill to renew its charter, 226; removal of deposits, 227; petitions for and against the removal of deposits, 228; power to create a, 235; "Fiscal" charter vetoed by Tyler, 256, 259, 260

Bankrupt bill, 261

"Bargain and Corruption" charge against Clay, 126–130

Benton, T. H., on Foot's Resolution, 158–160; cartoon of, 231; on Calhoun, 241

Berrien, John M., attacks Webster, 281

Berwyn, supports Webster, 235

Birney, James G., 242

"Bloody Bill," 203

Boscawen, Webster practises law at, 43–44

Boston, Webster speaks at, in 1835, 232; Whig convention at, 235; Garrison mobbed in, 242; friends in, tender Webster a dinner, 276; Webster speaks in, 276

Botts, Mr., "extraordinary" letter of, 259, 260

Brentwood, Webster at the convention, 63, 64; writes the address, 65–66

Buckminster, Joseph S., one of Webster's teachers, 15–16

Buffalo, visited by Webster, 240

Buffalo Creek, 264

Bunker Hill oration, 132–136; speech at Whig meeting, 251

Calhoun, John C., Webster on, 122; defeats tariff bill (1827), 147; writes "South Carolina Exposition," 156; address to the people of South Carolina, 194–195; letter to Gov. Hamilton, 195; Webster intends to answer it, 195–196; elected to the Senate, 203; resolutions on the Constitution, 204; debate with Webster, 210; on the basis of Southern Union, 241; Northern views of his objects, 242; presents a bill against antislavery literature, 243; resolutions of, on slavery in District of Columbia, 246; Webster's charges against, 248–249; resolution of, 250; extending the Constitution, 303–305

California, plan to buy, 282

Canada, rebellion in, 264; intended invasion of, 269

Caroline affair, 263–270, 272, 273

Cartoons, 230

Cass, Lewis, letter to Webster, 267

Caucus of 1824, opposed by Webster, 114

Charleston, S. C., 242

Charlestown, Mass., Webster accused of burning the convent at, 252

Chester County, sends Webster delegates, 235

Chicago, visited by Webster, 240

Children of Webster, 48

Choate, Rufus, wishes to resign, 284; expiration of term, 285; succeeded by Webster, 288; Webster's influence over, 288; nominates Webster at Baltimore, 289; at Whig convention, 331

Cincinnati, visited by Webster, 239; mobs in, 242

Clay, Henry, on the tariff, 118; answered by Webster, 118; attack on, by Kremer, 126, 129–130; resolution to censure Jackson, 228; cartoon of, 230; supports Calhoun, 246, 247; Webster's charge against, 247, 248; resolution of, 250; offered the Department of State, 255; presented by a Massachusetts convention as a presidential candidate, 276; nominated by the Whig

B ✓

B WEBSTE, D.
McMaster, John Bach,
1852-1932.
Daniel Webster,

14489
31Jan'62

40386
28Jan'64

28310
4 Apr'64
28488
12 May'64
43932
9Jan'65
45200
17Apr'65

3398
11May'65
52095
17 Jan'67
4305
9 May '67

57124
9 Oct'68
1684
17 Apr'72
10838
10 May'72
16849
1 Jun'72

JAN 29 '83

FEB 04 1984
JAN 1 8 1985
SEP 2 4 1986

DEC 22 1987